The Breadth and Depth of the Atonement

The Breadth and Depth of the Atonement

The Vicarious Humanity of Christ in the Church,
the World, and the Self: Essays, 1990–2015

Christian D. Kettler

◆PICKWICK *Publications* • Eugene, Oregon

THE BREADTH AND DEPTH OF THE ATONEMENT
The Vicarious Humanity of Christ in the Church, the World, and the Self: Essays, 1990–2015

Copyright © 2017 Christian D. Kettler. All rights reserved. Except for brief quotations in critical publications or reviews, no part of this book may be reproduced in any manner without prior written permission from the publisher. Write: Permissions, Wipf and Stock Publishers, 199 W. 8th Ave., Suite 3, Eugene, OR 97401.

Pickwick Publications
An Imprint of Wipf and Stock Publishers
199 W. 8th Ave., Suite 3
Eugene, OR 97401

www.wipfandstock.com

PAPERBACK ISBN: 978-1-4982-8901-6
HARDCOVER ISBN: 978-1-4982-8903-0
EBOOK ISBN: 978-1-4982-8902-3

Cataloguing-in-Publication data:

Names: Kettler, Christian D., 1954–

Title: The Breadth and Depth of the Atonement : The Vicarious Humanity of Christ in the Church, the World, and the Self: Essays, 1990–2015 / Christian D. Kettler.

Description: Eugene, OR : Pickwick Publications, 2017 | Includes bibliographical references and index.

Identifiers: ISBN 978-1-4982-8901-6 (paperback) | ISBN 978-1-4982-8903-0 (hardcover) | ISBN 978-1-4982-8902-3 (ebook)

Subjects: LCSH: Jesus Christ—Person and offices. | Atonement.

Classification: BT265.3 .K48 2017 (print) | BT265.3 .K48 (ebook)

Manufactured in the U.S.A.   05/04/17

Scripture quotations are from the New Revised Version of the Bible, copyright © 1989, by the Division of Christian Education of the National Council of the Churches of Christ in the United States of America. Used by permission. All rights reserved.

The following essays were granted permission for republication:

Used by permission of Wipf and Stock Publishers. www.wipfandstock.com: "The Atonement as the Life of God in the Ministry of the Church," originally published in *Incarnational Ministry: The Presence of Christ in Church, Society, and Family: Essays in Honor of Ray S. Anderson,* edited by Christian D. Kettler and Todd H. Speidell, 58-77. Colorado Springs: Helmers and Howard, 1990.

"'For I Do Not Do the Good I Wish . . . And I'm Tired of Trying': Weakness and the Vicarious Humanity of Christ," originally published in *On Being Christian . . . and Human: Essays in Celebration of Ray S. Anderson,* edited by Todd H. Speidell. (2002).

Used by permission of *Edification: The Journal of the Society for Christian Psychology:* "Advocate and Judge: The Vicarious Humanity of Christ and the 'Ideal' Self," originally published in *Edification: The Journal of the Society for Christian Psychology,* 1, Issue 2, (2007).

Used by permission of Sage Publishing:

"The Vicarious Beauty of Christ: The Aesthetics of the Atonement," originally published in *Theology Today* 64, no. 1 (2007).

Used by permission of *Participatio, Journal of the Thomas F. Torrance Theological Fellowship,* www.tftorrance.org:

"He Has Seen the Stars for . . . Us: The Vicarious Humanity of Christ, the Priest of Creation," *Participatio: Journal of the Thomas F. Torrance Theological Fellowship,* Vol. 5 (2015), accessible at www.tftorrance.org.

To the Allison family: Dale, Kris,
Emily, Andrew, and John

Contents

Introduction | ix

1. The Atonement as the Life of God in the Ministry of the Church | 1

2. The Vicarious Humanity of Christ and Cultured Identity: Joy and Despair in an Age of Globalization | 24

3. The Vicarious Beauty of Christ and the Aesthetics of the Atonement | 35

4. God's Joy in Action: Creation Out of Nothing and the Vicarious Humanity of Christ | 47

5. He Has Seen the Stars . . . For Us: The Vicarious Humanity of Christ, the Priest of Creation | 66

6. "For I Do Not Do the Good I Want . . . And I'm Tired of Trying": Weakness and the Vicarious Humanity of Christ | 83

7. Image and Substitute: The Vicarious Humanity of Christ in a World of Genetic Engineering | 103

8. Advocate and Judge: The Vicarious Humanity of Christ and the "Ideal" Self | 114

Bibliography | 125

Index | 135

Introduction

A TONEMENT. FOR SOME, THIS word is the heart of the Christian faith. For others, it is irrelevant for Christianity and how they live their Christian lives. In recent years, many rose to its defense, particularly in its "penal substitutionary" form, that this is the center of the faith. Others have said quite the opposite; criticizing such a "violent" soteriology, and re-enforcing the long tradition of the cross as a "moral example," simply a demonstration of sacrificial love.[1] Both sides have elements of truth, I would contend. But do they present the richness, the breadth and the depth of the gospel of Jesus Christ? This is where I have found the understanding of the vicarious *humanity*, not just death, of Christ so illuminating. And so, this book, *The Breadth and the Depth of the Atonement: The Vicarious Humanity of Christ in the Church, the World, and the Self* is offered.

What began as a seminary student's awakening in the classes of Ray Anderson at Fuller Seminary developed at first into a PhD, "The Vicarious Humanity of Christ and the Reality of Salvation" at Fuller (1986). Even then I felt that such an understanding of the atonement had tremendous implications for areas into which the atonement rarely ventured. So after my dissertation was published (1991), previous books explored *The God Who Believes: Faith, Doubt, and the Vicarious Humanity of Christ* (2005) and *The God Who Rejoices: Joy, Despair, and the Vicarious Humanity of Christ* (2010). In between these years, I have written various essays and given papers on the vicarious humanity of Christ. These essays and papers consist most of this volume.

---

1. See the survey of atonement theories and debates between contemporary advocates in *The Nature of the Atonement: Four Views*, edited by James Beilby and Paul R. Eddy.

INTRODUCTION

What was it that attracted and still attracts me to the doctrine of the vicarious humanity of Christ? Perhaps because it resonates so strongly with the Christian reality of *grace*. This was so important to me as an alienated teenager coming to faith. I did not need to bring popularity or achievement, but "simply to the cross I cling." My first pastor, Bob Myers, certainly impressed that upon me. Whatever misgivings I have now about the dispensational theology he received at Dallas Seminary, one thing Bob hammered on to us kids was precious: grace. My subsequent discovery of Karl Barth only reaffirmed this. Many would say that the Protestant tradition in which I was reared is too much filled with what Dietrich Bonhoeffer called "cheap grace."[2] Certainly that can always be a danger. Yet my experience of grace has been so overwhelming that what James Torrance said many times has always remained true for me: "Unconditional grace means unconditional obligations." Was that not true for "the father of faith," Abraham? Indeed, was that not true for the faith (vicarious?) of Jesus himself? As I entered my twenties, with new trepidations and anxieties, the understanding that Jesus Christ was not only the revelation of God, but also the foundation of our human responses, including faith, was liberating and dynamic. It started me on a lifetime theological quest to understand its "breadth and depth."

A word about the outline of this volume: Although the section on "Church" is only one article, the fact that it begins these essays demonstrates the church's foundational place. The church of Jesus Christ, the body of Christ, is the *place* where the atonement is realized, where it refuses to be abstract, where it is connected dynamically to the continuing ministry of Jesus Christ. Nonetheless, the vicarious humanity of Christ teaches us that the implications of the atonement widens out into *the world*, the second section, into such issues as dealing with culture and aesthetics. Still, even though *the self* is last in the order of this volume, it possesses the greatest number of essays. Why? Perhaps, despite (or because?) of the myriad of issues and choices that confront the postmodern self, the "breadth and depth" reaches deep into the individual who Christ calls to follow him, die, and live in union with him. Even "the church" and "the world" can be used to escape from that call to discipleship if one simply equates either church programs or the agenda of the world ("missing" the next step of "history") with the ministry of Christ.

In one sense, the central place of the forgiveness of sins in the first essay, "The Atonement as the Life of God in the Ministry of the Church"

---

2. Bonhoeffer, *Discipleship*, 43–56.

brings the reader full circle, from ending with the self whose sins are forgiven, back to the context in the church. Here, one must remember that although the forgiveness of sins is that which "the church can say that no one else can say" (John Leith), one must remember its relation to "the breadth and depth" of the atonement. I think I even saw this in my PhD dissertation, published as *The Vicarious Humanity of Christ and the Reality of Salvation*. The "depth" of salvation is seen in the cross, where Christ even "repents" for us.[3] Yet the subsequent chapters include both an eschatological reality in the world (the Epistle to the Hebrews) and Christ and the Last Adam and his relation to the church as the body of Christ in Paul.[4] As Ray Anderson has observed, forgiveness of sins goes beyond simply removing our "objective guilt" but leaving us spiritually powerless.[5] For the church to leave a person with only forgiveness of sins without power to overcome sins is "spiritual malpractice."[6]

In reviewing these essays and papers it occurred to me that the "breadth" and "depth" of their topics spoke of a wideness and richness to the vicarious humanity that needs to be expressed. The first essay, "The Atonement as the Life of God in the Ministry of the Church" does speak of the atonement, however, in its practical, concrete place in *the church*, not just in a theory. In a sense it frames all of the other essays and their place irrevocably in the church of Jesus Christ, his body, and his ministry. Yet that church goes out into *the world*, as the second part of the essays makes clear, and the atonement as the vicarious humanity of Christ has intriguing possibilities with it: culture in an age of globalization, aesthetics and beauty, the doctrine of creation, and Christ as the priest of creation are all explored. And then, lastly, the vicarious humanity of Christ does not allow us to forget *the individual self*, dealing with one's emotional weaknesses, being questioned what is a self in an age of genetic engineering, and even quickly falsely seeking to satisfy oneself in a quest for an "ideal" self.

The harvest is ready. T.F. Torrance and his brother James, who articulated the doctrine of the vicarious humanity of Christ so well, have "planted the seed," as it were, and it is up for others to wrestle with the implications of what they have found in Scripture and the Christian tradition: the vicarious humanity of Christ. I have found the possibilities to be greatly rewarding.

3. Kettler, *The Vicarious Humanity of Christ and the Reality of Salvation*, 9, 187–204.
4. Ibid., 205–32; 263–88.
5. Anderson, *Dancing With Wolves While Feeding the Sheep*, 77.
6. Ibid., 75.

INTRODUCTION

Many thanks go to Bonnie Dexter, our administrative assistant, Michelle Quinones, our student assistant, bookstore manager Michael Sullivan, Willis Overholt, and the staff of Edmund Stanley Library of Friends University, for invaluable assistance.

Reading these essays again was like revisiting old friends. We have both changed, but when we see one another again, we encounter a richness that we never knew existed before. Therefore, it became only natural to dedicate this book to old friends I have cherished through many years, the Allison family: Dale, Kris, Emily, Andrew, and John.

CHAPTER ONE

The Atonement as the Life of God in the Ministry of the Church

IN THE HEART OF his seminal essay, "A Theology for Ministry," Ray S. Anderson states the guiding thesis of his theology of ministry: "Ministry precedes theology and produces theology, not the reverse."[1] The various contributions that Dr. Anderson has made to the continuing discussion on the integration of theology and ministry consistently reflect this thesis. The theologian does not construct a speculative mansion which the church should be forced to inhabit. There is no intellectually snobbish lordship which theology should possess to determine the ministry of the church. Anderson can be misunderstood, however, if one does not pay close attention to what he means by "ministry": "Ministry is determined and set forth by God's own ministry of revelation and reconciliation in the world, beginning with Israel and culminating in Jesus Christ and the Church."[2] So Anderson's call is not to surrender to the banalities of an obsession with techniques, fueled by pop psychology and the theologically questionable belief that the "consumers" in the church and in the world know what they "want" and so the church, as a good supplier, should deliver the product according to supply and demand. No; the ordered priority of ministry before theology for Anderson means that God's own ministry, revealed by his act of grace, first in Israel, then fulfilled in Jesus Christ, is an act of revelation and reconciliation on behalf of a needy world. God has his own ministry, and the church as the body of Christ is simply obligated to enter into and

1. Anderson, "A Theology for Ministry," 7.
2. Ibid.

participate in the continuing ministry of Jesus Christ out of God's grace alone.

Theology then follows this participation in the ministry of God. The purpose of this essay is to examine theologically one aspect of that ministry of God, the ministry of atonement from the sins of the world, and to seek to allow the reality of God's ministry of atonement and reconciliation to inform and shape the contours and content of the ministry of the church, what the church is to do and say. Several "dogmatic postulates" will be offered and then tested in order to suggest some modest, yet it is hoped important, conclusions.

Much of what follows seeks to build upon the provocative and evangelical epistemology of Karl Barth and Thomas F. Torrance. Wilhelm Pauck remarks that Barth's statement, "God is known by God and by God alone" is the essence of Barth's theological epistemology."[3] The statement does guide us into some of the far-reaching implications of the theology of Karl Barth, many of which are reflected in Ray Anderson's pioneering work on theology and ministry. The knowledge of God is, first of all, God's own knowledge. God possesses it. It cannot be the rightful possession of anyone else. If God is to be treated as God, it must be on his initiative if we are to truly know him. Thus theological epistemology is always an epistemology of grace. Knowledge of God, therefore, is not gained by "works righteousness," by our attempts to know God, in the same way that salvation is not gained by the merit of our works (Eph 2:8–9). Knowledge of God, as well as salvation, comes by God's initiative, God's grace, alone. In recent years, Thomas F. Torrance has shown repeatedly how this way of thinking is in harmony with the Einsteinian scientific method which allows the nature of what we seek to know determine the means by which we know it.[4] The connection to Anderson's thesis, "Ministry precedes and produces theology, not the reverse," is obvious: Ministry involves nothing less than the knowledge of God, if it is to be the ministry of Jesus Christ.

Despite Barth's notoriety, his contribution has been met, unfortunately, by responses similar to Wilhelm Pauck's: "What a strange idea it is, what a disturbing idea to be entertained and explained by a human mind!"[5] For

---

3. Barth, *Church Dogmatics* (cited afterwards as *CD*) II/1: 47 and Pauck, *The Heritage of the Reformation*, 354.

4. T. F. Torrance, *The Ground and Grammar of Theology*, 8.

5. Pauck, *The Heritage of the Reformation*, 354. Pauck shares the belief of Harnack that because of this "strange idea," Barth will inevitably think that he is the recipient of inspirations and end up founding his own sect (!). Ibid., 359.

as Pauck explains, this can only mean either that God is unknowable, since there is no "point of contact" between God and humanity, or that a human being can make the claim that his thoughts are identical to God's. The better alternative, Pauck says, is to construct a theology closely critiqued by the historical relativity of all theology, in the mode of Adolf von Harnack.[6] The *actuality* of the revelation of God is to become predicated on the successful investigation into the *possibility* of knowing God. Given the problem of the revelation of God in a pluralistic world with any number of highly divergent claims of revelation, from the Ayatollah to Jim and Tammy Bakker, such a historical critical approach is very attractive to the thinking person.

But as safe as this may sound for the academic, when we consider such topics as the relationship of the atonement to the ministry of the church, such a theology is found wanting. The preacher, for example, does not have the luxury of purely cold historical analysis, if one is to be a preacher of the Christian gospel. One cannot and should not qualify and relativize to death each utterance one makes, if God has truly revealed himself in Jesus Christ.[7] Christianity has never meant anything less than God's self-revelation when it has continued to be Christianity. "Ministry precedes theology"!

The *actuality* of revelation means a great deal when we consider the reality of reconciliation and atonement.[8] For if we believe that "God is known by God and by God alone," we must approach the question of what God *did* for us based on *who* he has revealed himself to be. This, in turn, can set the church free to determine its ministry based on *who* God is and what he has *actually* done, rather than what would sell in the marketplace of ideas and religions and in "self-help" books.

My proposal is that such a theological epistemology allows the doctrine of the atonement to be centered on the healing effect of the very *life* of God communicated to humanity in the life, death, and resurrection of Jesus Christ. This life cannot be known by us except through God's initiative. "God is known by God and by God alone"! And the Christian doctrine of

---

6. Ibid., 358–59.

7. Proclamation is the "presupposition" of theology, "its material and its essential goal, not its content or task." Barth, *CD* I/1, second edition: 51.

8. See also Barth on the priority of the reality of revelation over its possibility, *CD* I/2: 1–44. For Barth, this is integrally connected with his doctrine of God, as Torrance explains: "God is not another activity but *the* Actuality or Reality through which and in which our own actuality and that of the world is actuality—the *causa prima, ens realissimum,* and *actus purus,* the One Actuality that lies behind and is present in every other actuality. *Karl Barth, 1910–1934,* 154.

the atonement is based on nothing less than this, for it seeks to penetrate to the root of the human dilemma: human sin, which affects not just our behavior but even our ontological core. Certainly, other emphases on the atonement have been proposed in the history of the church. But purely external, forensic pronouncements of atonement, based on Christ paying the penalty for our sins, or a political restructuring under the idea of "liberation," are inadequate for the sake of the church's concrete ministry to actual people in actual crises of life. Such a ministry needs to be based on the *actuality* of God's revelation of grace. Only such a ministry is worthy of participating in the continual ministry of the Incarnate Son, Jesus Christ.

Both theological principles and ministry concerns will guide this investigation, which proceeds from four "dogmatic postulates" suggesting the actuality of God's gracious revelation and reconciliation in Christ. This is in order to tie more closely together who the church is and what it does with who God is and what he does, while maintaining Barth's dictum, "God is known by God and by God alone." These four assumptions are entitled: (1) "The heart of the Father as the beginning of the atonement," (2) "The incarnation of the Son as the ontological reality of the atonement," (3) "The vicarious humanity of Christ as the atoning Godward response on behalf of humanity," and (4) "The forgiveness of sins as the vivifying center of the actualization of the atonement in the life and ministry of the church." The implications of the doctrine of the atonement for the ministry of the church will be explored through use of a particular case study as a matrix in which to test these dogmatic postulates. If the ministry of Jesus Christ continues even today, indeed if revelation is *actual,* not just *possible,* then that ministry addresses the crucial pastoral issues confronting the ministry of the church. This is done not to offer facile answers to complicated situations, but to suggest how the ministry of Jesus Christ informs and directs our ministry in the church.

Our case involves Sondra, a woman of forty three who is wrestling with the effects of sexual abuse.[9] Starting at age five and continuing through age eleven, she was sexually abused by her father. When she was eleven her father was taken to court for abusing not only her but also her two brothers.

From ages eleven through twelve Sondra lived an outwardly normal life with her mother and brothers. But inwardly, feelings of shame, guilt, and family disgrace were pervasive. Sondra received no help during these

---

9. This case was provided by Sue Muhlenbruch, a graduate student in ministry at Friends University.

years. After she left home for college she knew that she needed professional care.

For the last twenty five years Sondra has sought help from both psychologists and spiritual leaders. About ten years ago, her father died. A hard and unforgiving spirit, however, still burns within her. Sondra has been married for twenty two years and has a teenage daughter. She sees no hope, no release from her memories. Her pastoral counselor at the local mental health clinic has told her that she needs to "become more spiritual." What has the doctrine of the atonement to say to Sondra? And how can that truth be mediated to Sondra through the life and ministry of the church?

The Heart of the Father as the Beginning of the Atonement

The atonement does not begin with the willingness of the Son to suffer and die, but with the heart of the Father (J. McLeod Campbell), the heart which refuses to let the world slide into the abyss of destruction. Thus, there is one divine purpose of love which is expressed in the Father's desire to rescue humanity from its own devices.

The *actuality* of revelation and reconciliation as the ministry of God begins with Jesus Christ as the Son of God. Why not the Father? Why not the Holy Spirit? The *incarnation* of the Son makes the difference. The true "point of contact" between God and humanity is the man Christ Jesus (1 Tim 2:5). But this Son is dependent upon the Father, according to the Gospel record. In the Fourth Gospel Jesus proclaims, "Truly, truly, I say to you, the Son can do nothing of his own accord, but only what he sees the Father doing" (John 5:19; Cf. John. 5:17,26,30,36; 6:37,44,57; 8:16,18,29; 10:18; 12:49). The revelation of the Son immediately becomes the revelation of the Father. There is a mutual knowledge between the Father and the Son: "No one knows the Son except the Father, and no one knows the Father except the Son *and anyone to whom the Son chooses to reveal him*" (Matt 11:27). Clearly this passage shows that not only is the incarnation our access to the Son, but also that the incarnation of the Son *truly reveals the Father.*

In some theories stressing the penal aspect of the atonement, the Son paying the penalty for humanity's sins at the hand of the Father's wrath has been emphasized to the point of denying de facto the unity of being between the Father and the Son. For some lay people this has had disastrous results.

This was true among the parishioners of the church of John McLeod Campbell, the great nineteenth-century Scottish theologian. McLeod Campbell had seen his people develop an idea of a great chasm between the wrathful Father and the innocent Son. In essence, God was the wrathful avenger of the sin which dishonored him and Jesus the innocent victim, appeased this wrath. This created among McLeod Campbell's parishioners an unrelieved fear of God the Father in contrast to the loving sacrifice of the Son. How could one be sure that the awesome wrath of the Father would be stayed?

Admittedly, this was a greater problem in the nineteenth century than it would be in most churches today. However, McLeod Campbell suggests a model of how a pastor becomes a theologian in order to provide *theological* answers to the problems of his people.

In response to his congregation's anxieties, McLeod Campbell worked out his view of the atonement in his major work, *The Nature of the Atonement* (1867). He perceived that a dualism had been created by the tradition of penal substitution so that the wrath of the Father was viewed in utter antithesis to the loving, willing innocence of the Son. What had purported to be an orthodox doctrine in effect denied the *homoousion* of the Nicene Creed, that the Son is of one substance with the Father. The New Testament, McLeod Campbell argued, presents the Son as the manifestation of the heart of the Father, a heart that refuses to allow humanity to drown in its own mire but is determined to rescue his creation. This is what salvation is all about:

> The question of salvation is seen to be sharply the question of participation in that favour as it is an outgoing of a living love, the love of the Father's heart, and not as the mere favourable sentence of a judge and a ruler, setting the mind at ease in reference to the demands of the law of His moral government.[10]

What of Sondra and her past? If God is simply the Judge and Ruler, how can the forgiveness of Christ become for her a forgiveness that breaks through even the encrusted pain and bitterness of the years? From the beginning, the act of the atonement comes from the heart of the Father, so that the importance of the *homoousion* and its relation to the atonement for pastoral care cannot be overestimated. The God who meets Sondra in the face of Jesus Christ with forgiveness and mercy is the same as God the

---

10. Campbell, *The Nature of the Atonement*, 220.

Father.¹¹ There is no "God behind God." As McLeod Campbell states, there is one divine purpose of love seen in the relationship between the incarnation and the atonement.¹²

The objection is often raised, however, that it is the demand of God as Judge of sin that gives the atonement the force of a moral imperative. The judge has pronounced the verdict, so *the law* should lead one in living the Christian life.¹³

At first glance, it does appear that the judge has more "power" over the "convicted criminal" than the accused's "father" does. But is this really so? R. S. Franks commends McLeod Campbell for his insight at this point. In fact, states Franks, the demand of a judge is really less morally demanding than the demand of the father. The judge is only interested in justice being done. But the father presents a continual demand on his son because of that filial relationship. The command of a parent who is known by the child to love the child dearly, who has provided for the child in many sacrificial, costly ways, has an infinitely greater influence on the child's behavior than the cold letter of the law could ever hope to have. The heavenly Father, therefore, demands nothing less than "a complete and perfect holiness of life.¹⁴

This is not to rule out the Father's wrath against sin and the rightful place of the law in the Christian's life. Nonetheless, the "filial" *precedes* the "judicial" in McLeod Campbell's thought, as James Torrance observes.¹⁵ Apart from this sense of the *origin* of the atonement in the heart of the Father, can the church's preaching, teaching, or pastoral care hope to break through Sondra's bitterness?

But, it might be asked, would a theology based on God as "Father" be truly helpful to a woman like Sondra, who has been abused by her own father? Would it not be better for Sondra simply to refer to God as "Creator" or even "Mother," as many have suggested?

---

11. T. F. Torrance tells of his moving experience as a chaplain on the battlefield when a young man, dying, asked him, "Will God really turn out to be what we believe him to be in Jesus Christ?" The importance of the *homoousion* for pastoral ministry could not be more vividly portrayed. T. F. Torrance, *The Mediation of Christ*, 59.

12. Campbell, *The Nature of the Atonement*, xix.

13. This is a common deduction from Calvin's use of the law in the life of the believer. Calvin, *Institutes*, 2.7.12–13; 2.9.3.

14. Franks, *The Work of Christ*, 671–72.

15. James B. Torrance, "The Contribution of John McLeod Campbell to Scottish Theology," 311.

A theological epistemology such as Barth's ("God is known by God and by God alone") can help us to recognize this problem while avoiding an answer that may create unwanted consequences. "God is known by God and by God alone" prohibits us from reading into God any idea of God, including our ideas of "father." This needs to be communicated to Sondra and it can be, if we maintain that the knowledge of God the Father originates from our knowledge of the Son, Jesus Christ (Matt 11:27). To read maleness into God because he is called Father is only to read *our* ideas of fatherhood into God. The second commandment, along with the rest of the biblical tradition, clearly forbids this (Exod 20:4; Cf. Deut 4:15–16). Again, an epistemology of grace has great implications for what extent the healing power of the atonement can work in the personal crises of men and women. At stake here is the importance of "incarnate particularity," as Roland M. Frye puts it.[16] T. F. Torrance makes the case clearly that what is at stake is nothing less than a sure knowledge of God:

> We cannot know God behind his back, as it were, by stealing knowledge of him, for we may know him only in accordance with the way he has actually taken in revealing himself to us. Hence, as Hilary has shown so well, we can only make use of the analogies and terms which God himself has posited, and which he has linked to his self-revelation so that they point beyond themselves. It is in this way we interpret expressions like 'father' and 'son.'[17]

Sondra needs to know the healing power of the Son—the genuine, historical Jesus of Nazareth, the one who reveals the heart of God the Father. A strictly penal view of the atonement, as we have seen, can project a purely forensic view of God the Father as only a judge. The solution is not to abandon the analogy, but to allow the biblical witness to define its content, as McLeod Campbell recognized. This is also true concerning the "maleness" of God the Father.

The Incarnation of the Son as the Ontological Reality of the Atonement

The atonement is not simply one moment of time on the cross, but the "development" of the incarnation, of the heart of the Father revealed

---

16. Frye, *Language for God and Feminist Language*, 6.
17. T. F. Torrance, *Reality and Scientific Theology*, 201 nn. 3–4.

> *in the Son, who has partaken of human flesh. Therefore, atonement is essentially the ontological communication of the life of God, a life that gives itself in suffering love, even to the pain of death on a cross.*

The heart of the Father has healing and atoning effects when it lives in the life of the Son. As McLeod Campbell puts it so well, the atonement is the "development" of the incarnation in an "indissoluble way," as a "natural, not arbitrary relationship" between the Father and the Son. What we have revealed here is nothing less than the stupendous fact that, in the incarnation of the Son, humanity participates in "the history of the inner life of His Godhead" (Barth).[18] God communicates his own life in order to heal broken humanity. Again, "God is known by God and by God alone." As we have seen, to Wilhelm Pauck this is a "strange and disturbing" idea, but to hurting people like Sondra it could be the beginning of the way back to emotional and spiritual health.

Despite much of the current interest in "spiritual formation," "the inner life," and spiritual "disciplines," which too often focus on our own piety, perhaps the greatest resource for spiritual formation is found rather in *God's* "inner life." It is the "inner life" of God as Trinity, one God in three ways of being-Father, Son, and Holy Spirit- that has been revealed to us in the Christian gospel. Indeed, has that not always been the amazing significance of the doctrines of the Trinity and the incarnation? Healing and reconciliation come when we participate by the Spirit through faith in this "inner life" of the triune God, made manifest to us by the incarnation of Jesus Christ.

This is not to say that the inner life of humanity is unimportant. In fact, the manifestation of the inner life of God in Jesus Christ desires a radical surgery on humanity, an *ontological, internal* salvation, aimed at the root cause of the human predicament, sin. This, of course, has to *begin* with the individual's inner life. The psalmist certainly was aware of this when he prayed, "You desire truth in the innermost being" (Ps 51:6). Despite contemporary obsessions in the church with "social justice" and emotional coping and, therefore, with *external* behavioral change, *inwardness,* change at the root of ontological existence, is the beginning of following Jesus, according to the Gospels.

Jesus' teaching is plain and repeated on the folly of what we might call "surface atonement." An example would be his criticism of parading one's piety before others (Matt 6:1.). In contrast to such a display, he exhorts his listeners to give attention to what truly "defiles" a person; "the things which

---

18. Barth, *CD* IV/1: 215.

come *out* of a man are what defiles him" (Mark 7:15). At the heart of the Sermon on the Mount is Matthew 6, which Dietrich Bonhoeffer entitles, "The Hidden Character of the Christian Life."[19] Certainly one should not ignore the external and outward manifestations of a disciple of Jesus. The Sermon is also plain concerning that: "You are the light of the world . . . " (Matt 5:14). But does not Jesus' teaching on inwardness call us to regard the *beginning* of the atoning act of Christ as a radical surgery on what is *within the individual,* and only subsequently with implications for the external and social life? In fact a biblical paradigm seems to be repeated through Scripture that emphasizes the act of God beginning from an *individual* for the sake of the larger *community* (or from the *particular* to the *universal*). Abraham is chosen by Yahweh so "by you all the families of the earth shall bless themselves" (Gen 12:3). The Servant in Isaiah is given as "a covenant to the people, a light to the nations" (Isa 42:6). And, of course, Jesus creates a community, the twelve, then the church, to "make disciples of all nations" (Matt 28:19). The larger community is not to be ignored, but the ontological nature of salvation begins with the particular, leading to the universal.

Such a temporal priority of the particular before the universal addresses *the root cause* of the human predicament and seems to be typical of Jesus, in contrast with many "surface" theories of the atonement and salvation. Whether they emphasize political restructuring (liberation theology), or the satisfaction of God's defaced honor (Anselm), or emotional coping (pop-psychology projects), or the disintegration of the self into God (pantheistic mysticism), these are inadequate in dealing with sin and its legacy for the human being. That is why Scripture speaks of Christ as our *life*. "I am the *life*" (John 14:6; 11:25). Paul's words are familiar: "To me to *live* is Christ" (Phil 1:21), and "Christ who is our *life*" (Col 3:4). In fact, Bonhoeffer can speak of Christ's life as "the origin, the essence and the goal of all life and of our life."[20] Christ not only pays the penalty for our sins, but also gives us the positive contribution of his very life.

---

19. Bonhoeffer, *The Cost of Discipleship,* 172. Davies and Allison note a parallel between Matt 6:1–6, 16–18 and Rom 2:28–29: "For he is not a real Jew who is one outwardly, nor is true circumcision something external and physical. He is a Jew who is one inwardly and real circumcision is a matter of the heart, spiritual and literal. His praise is not from men but from God." They conclude that the two passages reflect the pervasiveness of a "common Christian tradition," which was indebted to ancient Judaism. Davies and Allison, *Commentary on the Gospel According to Saint Matthew,* Vol. 1, 576.

20. Bonhoeffer, *Ethics,* 218.

Where is that life for Sondra? Where is she to find the life of Christ which can begin to deal with the depths of her anguish? Her pastoral counselor has told her that she needs to become "more spiritual." But the "spiritual" can be just as much a "surface" atonement, an excuse for idiosyncratic reclusiveness, unless there is an *incarnational place* for Sondra to begin to be healed.

Jesus' presence was such a place for the disciples. The church as the body of Christ, as the community of the atonement, should be a place of "rehabilitation" for all, building upon the accomplished radical surgery performed by the life of the Son lived in our human flesh. The inwardness of the atonement means that Sondra's individuality needs to be respected and nourished. The root of sin is *within* the individual, and to bypass the individual for "structural sins" is to be concerned only for the symptoms and not the disease typical of "surface atonements." In order for that individuality to be nurtured, the community is not to be a tyrant, but a place where Sondra can "recover" from the radical surgery of the atonement.

This understanding of community means that the church should be patient with Sondra—allowing her time to forgive her father and for her memories to be healed—and not expect her to be "healed" immediately. In fact, that very patience (grace) of the church becomes a judgment on Sondra's own sins. Perhaps the most basic issue in the contemporary discussion on the reality of physical healing gifts in the church today is *not* the question of whether such gifts remain in effect today, but rather the question of whether or not the church is prepared to be a place of "rehabilitation" for those whose healings, whether they be spiritual, physical, or emotional, may take years. This seems questionable as long as the church is obsessed with mere survival, whether through "church growth" techniques or simply in reflecting a certain political party's agenda.

In stark contrast, Ray Anderson even suggests that the church should be seen as a "hospice," a place where one can die with dignity and humanity.[21] If the radical surgery of the atonement involves the disturbing, even violent, metaphor of "dying with Christ" (Rom. 6:8), then should the church, as Christ's body, be anything less?

---

21. Anderson, *Theology, Dying, and Death*, 157

The Vicarious Humanity of Christ as the Atoning Godward Response on Behalf of Humanity

> *The atonement as the communication of the life of God for the sake of humanity's healing and reconciliation* is not only a "humanward" act but also a "Godward" act. *This* is *only proper if the atonement reaches into the depths of human existence in order to restore the whole person to God and to others. But at the heart of the human dilemma is the inability to respond to God with the proper response of perfect obedience. The doctrine of the atonement means that in the vicarious humanity of Christ, the entirety of Christ's life, culminating in his death on the cross, provides an atoning response of perfect worship, trust, service, and confession of sins to the Father on the behalf of humanity.*

The atonement of Jesus Christ reaches into the ontological depths of human existence. God is satisfied with nothing less than this. As such, the atonement nevertheless remains a mystery. For at its essence is the interplay of both our existence and God's existence, our being and God's being. This is the essence of atonement. Human existence must be involved in the atonement. As R. C. Moberly points out, atonement is not real unless it affects who I am.[22] The "legal fiction" of a purely forensic acquittal of sins does not help Sondra, whose very capacity for life, for joy, for service, for love has become severely crippled by the bitterness of the years. Nor would simply a cheap, sentimental word of forgiveness mean anything to Sondra's *being*, a being trapped in sin and death. As B. A. Gerrish notes, McLeod Campbell's view of the atonement should not be mistaken for such a Socinian view that "God's readiness to forgive makes atonement."[23] This does not mean, however, that God needs to be "propitiated" in the sense of being "moved to compassion." It does mean that an action is needed in time and space in order to help rescue humanity from its ontological state of sin. God's existence must be involved in the atonement; but his being remains a mystery, even with the incarnation. When Karl Barth describes the significance of the virgin birth, he speaks of God's "inconceivable act of redeeming wisdom in which He completely assumes His creature in such a way that He imparts and bestows on it no less than His own existence."[24]

---

22. Moberly, *Atonement and Personality*, 137–38.
23. Gerrish, *Tradition and the Modern World*, 82.
24. Barth, *CD* I/1, second edition: 201. The parallels between Barth's thought and the thought of the Greek Fathers on deification *(theosis)* are obvious. Cf. Ware, *The Orthodox Church*, 236–42.

"No less than His own his own existence" -can one even begin to fathom such a fact? God's existence in the incarnation remains a mystery; or, as a true revelation of God ("God is known by God and by God alone"), it is a revelation we cannot master in all of its depth. The miracle of the virgin birth, Barth reminds us, is a sign of the mystery of God's act in the incarnate Son. "God is known by God and by God alone"!

The atonement does not end, however, with the communication of God's existence (Barth), for it must also be an act that takes place in *our* existence (Moberly). For God has created humanity to respond to his *address*, his *Word*. As Eduard Thurneysen declares, "God not only calls him [humanity] into being, but by calling him into being he summons him."[25] Because he is summoned, this creature is able to answer. Only those creatures who are summoned by God can answer. As Thurneysen continues, "God creates man not only *by* the Word; he creates him also *for* the word."[26]

But whatever the privilege of being addressed by God, humanity faces two dilemmas: (1) *How* does the human being respond to God? (2) *Can* the human being respond to God? Indeed, the refusal of humanity to acknowledge these dilemmas may be said to be the source of religion. One of the enduring contributions of Barth's early theology is his continual reminder that religion is the sinful person's attempt to respond to God, but only on the sinful person's terms. The tragic irony of the phenomenon of religion is that what appears to be an act of devotion is, quite the contrary, an act of supreme *hubris*.[27] In fact, the very reality of God becoming human in order to offer a perfect, obedient response argues against our meager attempts at responding, filled as they are with ulterior motives.[28]

At an existential and pastoral level, Sondra's inability to forgive her father reminds us that when her psychological "character armor" (E. Becker) is destroyed, she is not able to respond as she knows she should. Sondra knows that she should forgive her father. But the bare knowledge that one *should* do something does not necessarily empower the person to do so. The Kantian moralist may dogmatically assert, "I can because I ought," yet

25. Thurneysen, *A Theology of Pastoral Care*, 59. Cf. Barth, *CD* III/2: 147; Anderson, *On Being Human*, 33–43.

26. Thurneysen, *A Theology of Pastoral Care*, 59.

27. Barth, *The Epistle to the Romans*, 136, 206, 229, 276, 332, 368.

28. The extent of Christ's vicarious humanity may even extend to vicarious *repentance*. See the discussion in Kettler, "The Vicarious Repentance of Christ in the Theology of John McLeod Campbell and R.C. Moberly," 529–43 and Kettler, "Vicarious Humanity as Soteriology Reality," *The Vicarious Humanity of Christ and the Reality of Salvation*, 187–204.

the "post-conversion" interpretation of Romans 7 reminds us of human inability in the face of moral knowledge: "I do not do what I want, but I do the very thing I hate" (v. 15).[29] The implications for pastoral care are profound, as Thurneysen comments: "The pastoral counselor, directed by the Word of God, must know and remember throughout the whole conversation that moral conflicts cannot be worked out morally."[30] In effect, Sondra must not be cast back on her own "morality."

For this reason, in recent years Thomas F. Torrance has written frequently on the doctrine of the vicarious *humanity* (not just vicarious *death*) of Christ as an essential aspect of the atonement.[31] The vicarious humanity of Christ is an all-encompassing term that includes the totality of Christ's atoning life, including and culminating in his death on the cross. Still, the gracious act of God on behalf of humanity is not limited simply to one moment of time on the cross. It is true that, in that moment, Christ takes our place and represents us at the extremity of our death. "The wages of sin is death" (Rom 6:23; Gen 3:3). The atonement does include a substitutionary *death*, but this should be regarded only in the wider context of his substitutionary *life*. For atonement is not simply the act of God in saving humanity *from* sin, death, and hell, but also the act of God in saving us *for* eternal life, with all the fullness of the meaning of that reality.[32]

This is what Sondra needs to hear from the pulpit of her church. All of her desires to forgive her father have already been fulfilled in the genuine humanity of Jesus Christ, the one perfect response to the Father in, as T. F. Torrance declares, "trusting and obeying, understanding and knowing, loving and worshipping" and, we may add, forgiving.[33] As the Epistle to the Hebrews puts it so frankly, Christ was "made like his brethren in every respect," becoming a high priest and expiation for sin, to the extent of "learning obedience" by suffering (5:8, 2:10), even with "loud cries and tears" (5:7).[34] In like manner, the atonement penetrates into every point of

---

29. Thurneysen, *A Theology of Pastoral Care*, 285.

30. Ibid., 142.

31. Torrance's doctrine of the vicarious humanity of Christ is particularly emphasized in *The Mediation of Christ*, especially in chapter four, "The Mediation of Christ in Our Human Response." Cf. James B. Torrance, "The Vicarious Humanity of Christ" and Kettler, *The Vicarious Humanity of Christ and the Reality of Salvation*, 121–54 providing a summary and discussion of Torrance's doctrine.

32. Bultmann, "ζάω," 865.

33. T. F. Torrance, *God and Rationality*, 145

34. According to C. Spicq, the identification of Christ with humanity in every respect best expresses the content of the epistle. *L'Épître aux Hèbreaux*, I. 52.

Sondra's existence. As Calvin comments on Hebrews, in Christ are found all the qualities of human nature, even the "emotions of the soul . . . fear, dread of death, and the like" (Heb 4:15, 5:7–10), yet in the context of a perfect obedience (see the reference to Jesus' "godly fear" [5:7] and obedience [10:5–10]).[35] He is therefore able to make continual intercession for humanity (Heb 7:25).

Sondra is not alone. Christ has identified with her anguish. In some mysterious way, the terror, the fear, the guilt, the hatred, the shame that Sondra feels for her father is being felt by Christ himself. Her anguish has become his anguish. "Everything has happened to us, but in the context of the person of the Son" (Barth).[36] Will Sondra hear that in the Word preached to her on Sunday morning, or will she be preached a Christ who is only a "moral example," or a "satisfaction for sin," *external* to Sondra's being?

This point should not be misunderstood. Along with most other theories of the atonement offered through the history of doctrine, these two have truth to them, but not on their own. Apart from the vicarious humanity of Christ, a "moral example" only creates frustration at not meeting up to that example, and gives no hope to those who have failed time and time again at forgiving. In like manner, is a "satisfaction for sins" for the sake of God's damaged honor helpful to Sondra *now*, in the midst of her predicament? In his vicarious humanity, Christ takes Sondra's tears and frustrations up to the Father himself, forgiving her father for his wickedness, in order to clear the way for Sondra, so that she might forgive him herself, and start a new beginning for herself.

The Forgiveness of Sins as the Vivifying Center of the Actualization of the Atonement in the Life and Ministry of the Church

The actualization of the atonement in the ministry of the church is in the proclamation of the forgiveness of sins. This is the one act which only God can do, so it is rightly regarded as the unique task of the church, the body of Christ, to proclaim and live. Forgiveness of sins is the atoning manifestation of the life of God, motivated by the heart

---

35. Calvin, *The Epistles of Paul the Apostle to the Hebrews and the First and Second Epistles of Peter*, 25–25

36. Barth, *CD* IV/1: 222.

> *of the Father, taking deep ontological roots in humanity through the incarnation, and perfectly fulfilled by the faithfulness of the vicarious humanity of Christ.*

The atonement of Jesus Christ consists of the healing and reconciling effect of his entire life, reaching its climax in his death. This life becomes healing as it takes root deep in our ontological existence, leaving no part of the human person unexposed by the light of the vicarious life of Christ. In this life, the heart of the Father is made manifest, proclaiming the amazing love of God toward sinners: the forgiveness of sins.

But this does not mean that the incarnation and the cross were "necessary" for God to forgive sins. As Eberhard Jüngel has shown, the "necessity" of God is an aberration of Western natural theology, based on a philosophical anthropocentric theology which attempts to control God by regarding him as the most necessary being.[37] So also the forgiveness of sins has been viewed as "caused" by the instrument of the cross, something external to God's own being. This is similar to the debate over whether, in the atonement, God is reconciled to humanity, or humanity is reconciled to God. Karl Barth has been criticized by some for not affirming the atonement as the means by which God's attitude toward humanity is changed.[38] But, in Barth's defense, has God's attitude ever been anything but an expression of grace, even going back to the very act of *creatio ex nihilo*?[39] Even his judgment is an aspect of his grace (Ps 89:28–37). It is humanity that needs to be changed, not God. The incarnation, as McLeod Campbell observed, was "a peculiar development of the holy sorrow in which He bore the burden of our sins."[40] It seems more proper, therefore, to speak of the atonement as the *manifestation*, rather than as the *cause*, of the forgiveness of sins.[41]

---

37. Jüngel, *God as the Mystery of the World*, 24–25. Such a tradition of the "necessity" of God contrasts sharply with the biblical doctrine of the contingent relationship between God and the world. "The baffling thing about the creation is that it came into being at all, and now that it has come into being it contains no reason in itself why it should be what it is and why it should continue to exist. Indeed God himself was under no necessity to create the universe." Thomas F. Torrance, *Divine and Contingent Order*, vii.

38. Wells, *The Search for Salvation*, 60.

39. Barth, *CD* III/2: 94, "Creation as the External Basis of the Covenant."

40. Campbell, *The Nature of the Atonement*, 136.

41. Does this imply universalism? Not particularly, if one remembers the judgmental nature of forgiveness. As James Torrance points out, the proclamation of forgiveness implies that the forgiven person is guilty. When one says "I forgive you," this is not only a word of love and reconciliation, but also of judgment. Whether or not the guilty party accepts that word is another question. "The Vicarious Humanity of Christ," 142–43.

Regardless of one's theology of the forgiveness of sins, it is hard to ignore its central place in the theology of the atonement. In the forgiveness of sins, we find the motive behind the atonement, the expression of the heart of the Father. The heart of the Father is simply God's desire to forgive our sins; and, indeed, forgiveness is an outworking of his eternal nature of love.

But some voices have recently asked whether the church today has forgotten this central place of the forgiveness of sins, and therefore has forgotten what "the church can say that no one else can say." Indeed, that is the subtitle of a recent book by John Leith, *The Reformed Imperative: What the Church Can Say that No One Else Can Say*.[42] In an age when social and political problems seem to attract the most attention from the mainline churches, Leith suggests that the church has readily surrendered its unique theological mission and competence in order to emphasize management skills, psychological therapy, and social-political pronouncements, all tasks that can be done better by others.[43] In effect, the church's ministry as participation in the one ministry of Jesus Christ has become trivialized.

Thomas Oden laments the same situation in regard to the very identity of the contemporary pastor. Pastors of today are expected to be management specialists, psychological therapists, and social workers, all professions in which they have not been trained. A crisis in pastoral identity and self-confidence has resulted, for no matter which of these functions the pastor performs, there is always a businessman, a psychologist, or a social worker who can do them better! At the same time, the pastor's unique calling as the minister of the Word and Sacrament receives second billing. A "hungry anxiety to accommodate to modernity," Oden claims, has created a "loss of clarity about ministry in our time."[44]

Such a situation has great implications for the place of the forgiveness of sins in the church. The proclamation of the forgiveness of sins is essentially "non-utilitarian" in the perception of the wider society. Like philosophy, in William James' description, it does not "bake any bread."[45] This is so, basically, because the forgiveness of sins cannot be *seen*. One can see the effects of physical healing, growth in church membership, a food bank for the homeless, or a political action committee. The forgiveness of sins is hardly so visible, since it is an action within God himself, in God's "inner

---

42. Leith, *The Reformed Imperative*.
43. Ibid., 14, 21.
44. Oden, *Pastoral Theology*, 3.
45. James, *Pragmatism*, 8.

life," which can be known only through God's grace. That is why Barth's theological epistemology is so strategic for the doctrine of the atonement and the forgiveness of sins. The "non-utilitarian" and "invisible" nature of the atonement is expressed well by the early Barth:

> The atonement which occurred in Him is an invisible atonement which is contrasted with any soul-and-sense relationship between us and Jesus as impossibility is contrasted with possibility, death with life, non-existence with existence.[46]

Such an emphasis on an "invisible atonement" has been criticized recently by Klaus Bockmuehl as promoting the unreality of God in the world.[47] The "non-observability" of salvation, Bockmuehl contends, plays right into the hands of the Marxists, who have enjoyed such success attracting people with their "gospel" of salvation in this world, a salvation that can be seen.[48] The alternative to Barth is a theology based on Scripture, which proclaims the acts of God in the world, and an emphasis on "experience of the reality of God."[49] As Bockmuehl points out, Barth, later in life, modified his early overemphasis on the transcendence of God, which almost totally excluded the immanence of God.[50] Bockmuehl's work rightly states that the reality of God in the world is an issue of utmost concern. A "kerygmatic" theology can easily degenerate into rhetoric without reference to the concrete reality of the past or the present. Does Bockmuehl himself, however, forfeit the importance of the ontological change in humanity brought about by the atonement, a change which is within, and therefore (at least initially) "invisible"? Should one simply surrender de facto to the Marxist materialist doctrine by seeking the center of salvation in this world, rather than in God? Also, particularly striking is the absence of a discussion of the problem of evil in a world in which Bockmuehl so readily discerns God's acts. One might also question a reading of Scripture which seems to regard God's "acts" apart from his "being," for it is the life of God, as we have seen, that effects atonement.[51]

---

46. Barth, *The Epistle to the Romans*, 160.
47. Bockmuehl, *The Unreal God of Modern Theology*.
48. Ibid., 108, 132–35.
49. Ibid., 117, 142.
50. Barth, *The Humanity of God*, 39.
51. In *The Vicarious Humanity of Christ and the Reality of Salvation*, I argue that this desire to locate the center of salvation in the world resulted in a slew of modern anthropocentric soteriologies. As an alternative, Torrance's doctrine of the vicarious humanity

"God is known by God and by God alone" locates the center of the atonement in God's own being, reflecting his feelings and actions toward humanity. That is why the opponents of Jesus protested when the carpenter from Nazareth pronounced the forgiveness of sins by saying, "Who can forgive sins but God alone?" (Mark 2:7). The forgiveness of sins is "hidden" in the heart of the Father, but made manifest in the proclamation of Jesus Christ. How difficult this is to communicate to the present generation is particularly evident when one considers how contemporary culture despises the "word," in its idolatry for the "image" of television and sexual attractiveness, as Jacques Ellul tirelessly preaches.[52] Forgiveness of sins seems cheap, second rate, irrelevant to pressing social needs, and is often regarded as "privatistic," "pietistic," or "individualistic," in contrast to "liberation," which is "communal" and "holistic." And so the slogans go on.

In a modern classic of the theology of ministry, *A Theology of Pastoral Care*, Karl Barth's long-time associate Eduard Thurneysen makes an attempt to return the forgiveness of sins to the center of pastoral care, and, indeed, to the center of the ministry of the church. Much of pastoral care, Thurneysen contends, is weak and ineffectual because it is not regarded as "a communication of the Word of God" in a particular form, and especially as "the proclamation of the forgiveness of sins."[53] For in the forgiveness of sins, Thurneysen argues, we find nothing less than the very *power* of pastoral care: that is, the power of God's grace to reclaim the sinful world through Jesus Christ.[54]

Thurneysen has been criticized for being "unnecessarily restrictive" in confining all pastoral care to forgiveness.[55] But it seems that Thurneysen is onto something important. What often happens in the church, unfortunately, is that we give lip service and nod our heads to the *past* act of Christ's forgiveness, centering only on the cross, and forget about the implications of God's *continuous* life of the vicarious humanity of Christ in the church, a life of continual forgiveness. This is where our ecclesiology needs to be reshaped by the interrelationship between the vicarious humanity of

---

of Christ is suggested as a way to take seriously salvation in the midst of humanity and the world (vicarious humanity), while maintaining its origin and reality in God's inner life.

52. Ellul, *The Humiliation of the Word*.
53. Thurneysen, *A Theology of Pastoral Care*, 52–53.
54. Ibid., 67.
55. Tidball, *Skillful Shepherds*, 235.

Christ and the forgiveness of sins. Without going back to sacerdotalism, the church, as the body of Christ, needs to acknowledge that Christ has chosen to use the church as the expression of his vicarious humanity, for the sake of both the church and the world.

A fascinating example of how the vicarious humanity of Christ and the forgiveness of sins in the life and ministry of the church are woven together is found in the story of the healing of the paralytic and the pronouncement of the forgiveness of sins by Jesus (Mark 2:1-12; Matt 9:1-8; Luke 5:17-26). In Mark's version, Jesus is "preaching the word" to many (v. 2) when a paralytic is brought to him by four men. "And when Jesus saw *their* faith, he said to the paralytic, 'my son, your sins are forgiven'" (v. 5). (This is, interestingly enough, said *before* the event of Calvary!)[56] Some commentators follow Vincent Taylor and Calvin in explaining "their faith" in Mark 2:5 as including the faith of the paralytic as well.[57] Eduard Schweizer, however, in agreement with the ancient exegetes Victor of Antioch (fifth century) and St. Ephraem Syrus (fourth century), stresses the faith of the carriers alone as a sign that the act was entirely a work of God.[58] In fact, Ephraem notes the benefits of the "vicarious humanity" of the four carriers for the sick man: "See what the faith of others may do for one."[59] The possibility is there that "their faith" refers to the faith of the four men alone.

This argument is strengthened when one examines the six other stories of individual healing in Mark. In three out of the seven stories, some help is given by others to the one who is to be healed. (1) Concerning Peter's mother-in-law, *the disciples* "immediately. , . told him [Jesus] of her" (1:32). (2) "And *they brought to him*: a man who was deaf and had an impediment in his speech and *they besought him* to lay his hand on him" (7:32). (3) Concerning the blind man at Bethsaida: "And *some people brought to him* a blind man *and begged him* to touch him" (8:22); Cf. the crowd healing of 1:32.

This does not mean that "the vicarious humanity of Christ in the church" restricts the Holy Spirit's work in one way. God is still free to act as

---

56. Jesus says plainly that the sins of the man are forgiven at that moment, *pace* some writers such as R.S. Wallace: "He is asserting that he *has* the power to forgive only because he himself is on the way to meeting the full cost of forgiveness in the death he has come to achieve." Wallace, *The Atoning Death of Christ*, 23.

57. Taylor, *The Gospel According to St. Mark*, 194 and Calvin, *A Harmony of the Gospels, Matthew, Mark and Luke*, I, 258.

58. Schweizer, *The Good News According to Mark*, 61.

59. Cited by Swete, *The Gospel According to St. Mark*, 34.

he chooses. The healing stories in Mark that stress individual effort at seeking Jesus and the faith of the one who is to be healed remind us of that fact (1:40–45, 5:25–43, 10:46–52, and the crowd healing in 3:10). The combination of both elements in the crowd healing in 6:56 are particularly striking in this regard: "... *they laid* the sick in the market places, and *besought him that they might touch the fringe of his garment.*" Perhaps this should be a reminder that "the vicarious humanity of Christ in the church" is not an excuse for a "state socialism" in the church which denies the dignity and rights of the individual. Rather, the purpose of the vicarious humanity of Christ is to create a *basis* for individual faith.

Having seen "their faith," Jesus pronounces the forgiveness of sins for the paralytic. To the onlookers, Jesus was certainly not meeting the "needs" of the paralyzed man! But to prove that "the Son of Man has authority on earth to forgive sins," the paralytic was physically healed (vv. 10–12). In contrast to much talk today about a "holistic" approach to salvation, Jesus seems to give a priority to the forgiveness of sins over meeting physical needs. Now, one must quickly say that the physical need was met in time, but not at the expense of the forgiveness of sins. But can such a distinction between "spiritual" and "physical" be warranted, without making the church rich in words but poor in deeds?

In answer to this question, a reminder of a little noticed excursus in Barth's *Church Dogmatics* may be in order. No one can accuse Karl Barth of being simply a "privatistic" theologian, unconcerned with social or political ills. His stalwart opposition to Hitler's Germany speaks loudly against any such accusation. Nevertheless, in his discussion of the virgin birth, Barth has a very interesting excursus in which he defends the importance of the doctrine of the virgin birth by establishing its place as a "sign" of the incarnation, which is "the thing signified." The "sign," Barth claims, should never be confused with "the thing signified." The saving fact is the incarnation, not the miracle of the virgin birth. The forgiveness of sins and the physical healing of the paralytic are similarly related, he points out. The healing is a "sign," but it is not to be given priority over the pronouncement of the forgiveness of sins, "the thing signified."[60]

In Ray Bradbury's short story "Bless Me, Father, for I Have Sinned," a priest named Father Mellon is awakened at midnight on Christmas Eve by

---

60. Barth, *CD* I/2: 189. Barth's discussion of the hierarchy of the soul over the body is also interesting, given the contemporary tendency to homogenize the two and, in effect, ignore the importance of the soul. In contrast, Barth maintains the priority of the soul without ignoring the body and while considering the total person. Ibid., III/2: 338–40.

a peculiar urge to go down to the confessional of the church and wait. What he finds is an elderly penitent eager to spill the accumulation of sixty years of sins on the priest. The sins are personal, the kind that one would likely keep to oneself for years.

The last confession particularly jolts the priest. It involves a runaway dog named Bo, greatly beloved by the man when he was a young boy. For three days and three nights the dog had been gone, and the boy had given up hope. Then on Christmas Eve, at two in the morning, the boy heard the scratching of paws at the door. Bo was back! He grabbed the dog with great joy, calling his name over and over again. Then he suddenly stopped: "How dare he run away from me?" the boy asked himself. In hatred, the boy turned to the dog and beat him, while Bo just stood and took it all. "Oh, Father," the man cries to the priest, "he couldn't forgive me. Who was he? A beast, an animal, a dog, my love."[61]

The priest turns to the man and says that he, too, had the same thing happen to him. His dog had run off. He had hated his dog for leaving him. And upon the dog's return, he had beaten him. He had never told this to anyone, until now. A feeling of camaraderie develops, and the priest invites the man to share a glass of wine with him. But when he opens the confessional door, he finds the confessional empty. He has been talking with himself.

Even the priest needed a concrete person, a representative of the vicarious humanity of Christ, to hear his sins so that he, too, could receive forgiveness. So great was his need that he had to create the existence of that other person. "Confess your faults one to another" (Jas 5:16) is a call for the vicarious humanity of Christ to be operative in the church. While the Roman Church may be in error to restrict confession only to priests, Dietrich Bonhoeffer points out that oral confession is an imperative based on the vicarious humanity of Christ in the church: "Christ became our Brother in order to help us," Bonhoeffer says. "Through him our brother has become Christ for us in the power and the authority of the commission Christ has given to him."[62]

The atonement lives in the church when forgiveness of sins is given flesh in the presence of the brother or sister in the church–and not necessarily that of the pastor or priest. Eberhard Bethge recounts that one day in the Finkenwalde seminary, Bonhoeffer, who had encouraged his students

61. Bradbury, "Bless Me, Father, For I Have Sinned," *The Toynbee Convector*, 153.
62. Bonhoeffer, *Life Together*, 111.

to confess their sins to one another, asked one of the students to hear his own confession.[63] Like the priest, Bonhoeffer realized the need to know the forgiveness of sins through the touch of humanity, a humanity participating in the vicarious humanity of Christ.

The church could do many things for Sondra: provide psychological therapy, economic sustenance, or a community of service. But does not Sondra need to hear and feel and experience what the paralytic heard, "My son, your sins are forgiven," with all the implications of that stupendous announcement? The continuing life of God as the atonement can be communicated to Sondra through the church's acts of preaching, teaching, pastoral care, and fellowship. In these acts, the vicarious humanity of Christ continues to live in the church, the body of Christ, as we saw with the four men who carried the paralytic to Jesus: "And Jesus saw *their* faith." The paralytic was unable to carry himself to Jesus. The atonement continues to be powerful in the church when the message of forgiveness through the life of God is still proclaimed, even when we cannot believe, even when we need someone to believe for us.

Can the church dare to do this for Sondra? It can, if it allows its knowledge of God to come from God alone ("God can only be known by God and by God alone"), and therefore steadfastly determines to know no other gospel and no other ministry than the ministry of Jesus Christ. This can be done, not out of the church's own strength, but because the vicarious humanity of Christ, the manifestation of the life of God sent by the heart of the Father through the incarnation into the ontological depths of humanity, continues to live in a church that lives by nothing less than the forgiveness of sins.[64]

---

63. Bethge, *Dietrich Bonhoeffer*, 384.

64. Earlier versions of this essay were read by Dale Allison, Diane Ferguson, Bruce Parmenter, Todd Speidell, and Donna Van Haren. Their constructive comments were greatly appreciated.

CHAPTER TWO

The Vicarious Humanity of Christ and Cultured Identity

Joy and Despair in an Age of Globalization

MY GREAT-GRANDMOTHER, ANNA PRATTLE, arrived in Chicago from Bohemia with her named tagged to her dress. She hoped that someone would be there to meet her, for she spoke no English. But no one showed up. The fact that she did not speak the language of the country she had reached must have only accentuated the pain of anxiety when her expected greeter was not there. This seems to me to be a metaphor of two cultures meeting often repeated today: speaking different languages, often missing each other in the train station, not connecting. Where is Jesus Christ in this? Does either an orthodox divine-human Christology or a Jesus that reflects one's culture Christology say enough to this confusion? The encounter of cultures can be an occasion for despair, or for joy. This is all the more true for Christian theology, which both struggles to speak to the postmodern and non-western world but feels bound by its historical parochialism on one side and timid attempts to make Jesus "relevant" to culture on the other. How should Christian theology proceed if it is to be true to the gospel and sensitive to differing cultures?

My suggestion is to consider the implications of the doctrine of the vicarious humanity of Christ, as suggested in recent years by the Scottish theologian T. F. Torrance. While theologians have frequently spoken of the atonement as the vicarious *death* of Christ, Torrance suggests that the biblical testimony speaks of that death in the wider context of the vicarious *humanity* of Christ. Atonement, therefore, is not simply one moment of punishment on the cross, but found in the totality of the humanity that he assumed, our humanity.

The vicarious humanity of Christ encounters human culture because the Word became flesh (John 1:14). As such, God came in *solidarity* with humanity, including human culture. We can no longer speak of humanity, or individuals, apart from their culture. So also, we should not speak of the incarnation apart from an actual partaking in the creative "meaning-making" of culture (Stanley Grenz), the way human beings communicate and develop knowledge and attitudes of life (Clifford Geertz).[1] This includes religion. The vicarious humanity of Christ speaks of God embracing culture unconditionally: Jesus sitting at table with sinners and publicans. This is the movement downward, from God to humanity. All cultures, not just western ones, need to be affirmed as objects of God's unconditional love.

The gospel does not end with solidarity alone, however. There is a movement upward as well, from humanity to God. The goal of the vicarious humanity of Christ is the renewal of our humanity, to conform us to Christ's image, to be raised with Christ. All cultures, western and non-western, will need to be critiqued, then. This critique will be at the level where it may be the most painful to some of our most cherished ideas: our understanding of humanity, through our construction of a theological anthropology. Here is the place of the radical nature of the substitutionary atonement. Christ is not only in solidarity with humanity, but he is also our *substitute*. Christ as substitute displaces the self-willed agendas of humanity with his perfect faith, obedience, service, and even worship to the Father through the Spirit. Both romantic and imperialistic views of culture are judged by Christ the substitute. Yet Christ in substitution (the upward movement) is part of the one act of Christ that first involves Christ in solidarity (the downward movement). But can substitution be maintained without destruction of culture? Our failure to do so has led to many lamentable events in the history of Christianity.

We will further investigate this proposal by looking at, first, the problem of culture; secondly, the downward movement of solidarity; thirdly, the upward movement of substitution, and then fourthly, the agenda for the church of the vicarious humanity of Christ in culture.

---

1. Bourchard, "Culture," 121–22.

The Problem of Culture

First, the problem of culture: Culture is that remarkable paradox of human creativity and limitation, according to Charles Matthews.[2] Human beings create cultures, high and low, filled with their own values, expectations, and dreams. Creativity and freedom are kin to each other, and Kathryn Tanner can even argue that this suggests an openness to God.[3] We can at least admit that human beings are restlessly busy with their projects of what Stan Grenz called "meaning-making."[4]

They also find themselves born into a culture that one might feel alienated from, or oppressed by the power of another culture. There is not a pure or monolithic culture (a weakness in H. Richard Niebuhr's *Christ and Culture*), for cultures overlap and influence each other, even more so in the information age.[5] Religion is not to be isolated from culture, as we have long known from the nineteenth century work of Feuerbach and Troeltsch.

Yet most Christians find accommodation to culture troublesome. Despite the teaching in the Gospel of John that "God so loved the world," the first letter of John, along with other places in the Scriptures, exhorts the readers, "Do not love the world or the things in the world" (1 John 2:15). All Christians are suspicious about accommodation to culture, but we are of a divided mind concerning which aspects of culture are things indifferent and which should be shunned.[6] The tools of culture are gladly put to use by most: language, history, philosophy, social sciences, and popular culture. But again, the question remains of criterion: *Which* tools and *how* should they be used? Is it sufficient to say that, with William Dyrness, culture is "the continuing human response to God's ongoing project of reconciliation and renewal"?[7] Maybe another response is needed, the response of the vicarious humanity of Christ. If so, what does that response mean?

---

2. Matthews, "Culture," 46–52.
3. Ibid., 60.
4. Grenz, "Culture," 31.
5. Matthews, "Culture," 57.
6. Tanner, "The Religious Significance of Christian Engagement in the Culture Wars," 28–43.
7. Dyrness, *The Earth is God's*, xv, 58. Cf. Clifford Geertz: "We are, in sum, incomplete or unfinished animals who complete or finish ourselves through culture—and not through culture in general but through highly particular forms of it" (cited by Dyrness, 69).

The Downward Movement of Solidarity

Secondly, the downward movement of solidarity: The contemporary church tries mightily to be relevant to a postmodern culture, but frequently only betrays a lack of integrity and real concern for the humanity of the culture.[8] The desperate attempt to become relevant in a worship service consisting of nothing but a contemporary movie clip and a commentary is one example.

The first message of the incarnation is that God embraces humanity, welcoming sinners and eating with them (Luke 15:2), yet even though his presence at the table reveals the "perversion and corruption" of humanity.[9] In fact, Ray Anderson argues that, theologically, this is the first community Jesus created, not the church.[10] Sitting among a disreputable "culture" like the sinners and publicans, God has become as we are, "in the likeness of sinful flesh" (Rom 8:3), becoming accessible and knowable to humanity.[11] Culture is affirmed as a reflection of God's own freedom to create.[12] Solidarity should not be seen as God's abandonment of his deity, but God's desire for covenant with humanity. In Karl Barth's words, "God's deity does not exclude but includes His *humanity*."[13]

The epistle to the Hebrews speaks of Jesus enduring the cross, "for the sake of the joy set before him" (Heb 12:2). The solidarity of Christ with sinful humanity is a source of God's joy, a joy in participating in human "meaning-making," despite its wrong turns. This joy exists despite the despair caused by human sin, such as in the exploitation of one culture by another. God judges this in Jesus Christ. Hear Barth again: "The real goodness of the real God is that the contradiction of creation has not remained alien to Himself."[14]

Christian witness should reflect this kind of solidarity, in which the church meets a culture and allows the culture to minister to it, that sees brothers and sisters in the culture, not just potential converts. As Barth

---

8. Anderson, *An Emerging Theology for the Emerging Church*, 55.

9. Barth, *CD* III/2: 26–29.

10 Anderson, *Historical Transcendence and the Reality of God*, 227–37.

11. Barth, *CD* III/2: 53.

12. Barth, *The Humanity of God*, 39–44. Cf. Palma, *Karl Barth's Theology of Culture*, 59 and Barth, *CD* III/3:73 on the creature: "Its creation rested upon the free resolve of God; it was God's free act . . . And God was not under any obligation to cause it to come into existence and to be."

13. Barth, *The Humanity of God*, 49.

14. Barth, *CD* III/1: 380. Cf. Wood, *The Comedy of Redemption*, 48.

carefully elaborates, this kind of witness is in contrast to the kind of encounter that seeks "to invade and alter the life of my neighbor."[15] Solidarity is not just using communication skills but an acknowledgment that the Word has *already* become flesh, even judging the theology of the church. Who is the human being with whom God is in solidarity in Jesus Christ? Solidarity is with the cultures of all humanity, not just with the Christian and the individual believer's faith. I can only bear witness of my helplessness and the help I have been given by Jesus Christ that is available for all.[16] Solidarity begins to construct a theological anthropology based on the incarnation, fulfilled in the vicarious humanity of Christ. As deity and humanity are united, yet not confused in Jesus Christ (Chalcedonian Christology), so Jesus reveals the unity yet not confusion between soul and body in the human creature.[17] In this way the church is affirming that culture is a part of who we are, and therefore, is loved by God.

The solidarity of Jesus Christ with our humanity is also the first step in a critique of culture. We must be careful to hear what is being said: This is not simply a critique that reflects a perspective from a particular culture, such as a Hispanic perspective on Christology, as valuable as that may be. No, solidarity is only the first step in the very difficult (some would say inappropriate or impossible) critique of a culture. A critique, therefore, is best begun by one within the culture than from without. (President Barack Obama's critique of absent fathers in African-American culture comes to mind.) But this is what "the Word became flesh" of all human beings is all about. Christ speaks from within the culture of our humanity.

Solidarity is the essential first step, the downward act, of the incarnation. Yet how does solidarity keep from condoning uncritically all aspects of culture? Does acceptance mean a blanket approval of all facets of a culture? Here is the important place of the second movement of the incarnation, upward, in the vicarious humanity of Christ.

---

15. Ibid., *CD* I/2: 440–41. Cf. 441:"A witness is neither a guardian nor a teacher. He will not 'handle' him. He will not make him the object of his activity, even with the best intention. Witness can be given only when there is respect for the freedom of the grace of God, and therefore respect for the other man who can expect nothing from me but everything from God."

16. Ibid., *CD* I/2: 444.

17. Ibid., *CD* III/2: 341.

The Upward Movement of Substitution

Point three: the upward movement of substitution: Solidarity begins with the whole Christ taking on the whole of humanity—not just soul without body or the spiritual without the physical—including culture.[18] This will leads us irresistibly to substitution. Not one aspect of our humanity will escape being substituted by Jesus Christ.

The substitutionary atonement in terms of the vicarious humanity of Christ is first of all a critique that we do not want to hear. Many contemporary views of the atonement will gladly embrace Christ's solidarity with us but shy away from substitution. Could it be because we do not want aspects of our cultures touched by the gospel? Is this not just another way of saying that we do not want certain places in our lives to be touched by Jesus Christ? (My dear professor of historical theology, Geoffrey Bromiley, remarked once to me that the problem was not a lack of belief in substitutionary atonement, but that evangelicals did not believe in substitutionary atonement enough!) We may even retreat to a so-called "Christian worldview" that only joins Christianity with many competing worldviews and is ultimately a ripe example of postmodern relativism.

This critique, however, does not erase culture if it is preceded by solidarity. The "new creation" of Paul (2 Cor 5:17) is preferable to the transformation motif of H.R. Niebuhr.[19] We have been dead and we are now risen with Christ. (Rom 6). The writer of the first letter of John indicates in one sense that he is not writing a new commandment; it is in continuity with the old. "Yet I am writing you a new commandment that is true in him and in you, because the darkness is passing away and the true light is already shining" (1 John 2:7–8). Niebuhr agrees that the goal "issuing from Jesus Christ" is "an upward movement" to God, yet he lacks the ontological basis in the substitutionary response of the vicarious humanity of Christ.[20] Is this a case of being too easily pleased with "new wine in old wineskins"? The vicarious humanity of Christ (substitution) with its foundation in the downward precedence of solidarity speaks of a sure reality of dying and rising with Christ.

---

18. See H.R. Niebuhr's discussion of F.D. Maurice in *Christ and Culture*, 228.
19. Ibid., 194.
20. Ibid., 195–96.

The gospel is the declaration of both God's free grace and humanity's free gratitude, according to Karl Barth.[21] But our attempt at gratitude, even in our religions, has been judged wanting. We need someone to be "the perfect Eucharistic Being," in Alexander Schmemann's words.[22] This is the vicarious thanksgiving of Christ, a vicarious culture, if you will; a vicarious act that is not done apart from the first act of the downward movement: solidarity. Without both solidarity and substitution, the temptation, especially for religion, is to commit genocide; intellectually, politically, or socially. Examples from the Crusades to Croatia readily come to mind.

Christ as substitute needs to take the place of a culture that becomes an object of idolatry. In a sense, he frees culture from itself and its pretensions, even in attempting to respond to God. As in T. F. Torrance's critique of traditional natural theology, the problem with culture is not its existence, but its attempt to be independent of God.[23] Culture itself is provisional ("culturally conditioned") and lacks ontological status.[24] One needs to question the suggestion since the days of Paul Tillich that culture's creativity and freedom is a sign of openness to God. What we can say is that personal being in its awareness is by necessity open to something beyond itself. The awareness of our finitude is, as Polanyi and Torrance remind us, an awareness that we know more than we can say, but not an answer to that awareness.[25] William Dyrness can also be questioned when he suggests that one is "already embraced by the set of relationships that God sustains with the world."[26] He is understandably motivated by a doctrine of creation, yet creation can easily be disconnected from the christological insight that in Christ "all things in heaven and earth were created . . . all things were created through him and for him" (Col 1:16). Culture as creation is *for* Christ; in him culture finds its *telos,* its end, its purpose. Our perceptions and constructions of culture need to be critiqued by the double movement of the incarnation. This should include our perceptions of Christianity as well.

---

21. Barth, *The Humanity of God,* 47.

22. Schmemann, *For the Life of the World,* 38.

23. T. F. Torrance, *The Ground and Grammar of Theology,* 90. Cf. John Howard Yoder, "How H. Richard Niebuhr Reasoned," 70.

24. Palma, *Karl Barth's Theology of Culture,* 69.

25. T. F. Torrance, "The Social Coefficient of Knowledge," *Reality and Scientific Theology,* 110.

26. Dyrness, *The Earth is God's,* 68.

Culture is a part of human existence. So, from a Christian perspective, a theological anthropology is needed. Cultural anthropologists may hesitate to speak of what is means to be human, but the church should not fail to raise this question.[27] As Barth reminds us, the soul and body relationship should no longer, however, be viewed as separate from each other.[28] He may, like many modern theologians, go too far in denying these as two "substances."[29] One can respond that the two natures of Christ are considered to be "substances," two natures in one person. Yet he is right to view soul and body as a unity in terms of analogy to the hypostatic union between the divine and human natures of Christ, as the Council of Chalcedon in 451 A.D. hammered it out: not to be separated, but not to be confused. For our purposes, it is wise to continue to see the relationship in differentiation of the eternal triune being reflected in the double movement of the incarnation in both solidarity and substitution, not one without the other. So culture is affirmed, yet critiqued.

"Body is the openness of soul" according to Barth.[30] The human being "could not be a real person without this form and activity."[31] Through the expressions of culture, the body extends itself in creativity and freedom, but needs the direction of the openness and obedience of the Son to the Father through the Spirit.[32] True freedom is not in trying to alter one's nature but in true openness and obedience to one's source and destiny in God, as Bonhoeffer reminds us.[33] Might there not be a vicarious *culture* of Christ that is the continual upward movement of the Son, now expressed through the Holy Spirit, beginning to establish God's new creation?

The Agenda of the Vicarious Humanity of Christ for the Church in Culture

Fourthly, what is the agenda of the vicarious humanity of Christ in culture? What does it mean? What difference does it make? Can there be joy in the

---

27. Ibid., 64.
28. Barth, *CD* III/2: 405.
29. Ibid., 399, 417.
30. Ibid., 401.
31. Ibid.,, 418.
32. Ibid., 401.
33. Bonhoeffer, *Ethics*, 257, 284, 288.

midst of despair, as cultures collide, when, for example, even a Buddhist temple exists in Wichita, Kansas?

There is joy, I suggest, in the joy of the vicarious humanity of Christ, if it is understood to mean that there can be no solidarity without substitution and no substitution without solidarity; both downward and upward movements in the one act of the incarnation. A case in point may be the current conflict between traditional and contemporary worship in many American Protestant congregations, the so-called "worship wars." It is easy to see that this is a clash of cultures. The origins of "contemporary Christian music" go back to "the Jesus Movement," an international revival of the late nineteen sixties and early nineteen seventies (in which the present writer was a participant).[34] Whereas the theology was pure evangelical revivalism, with roots back to the nineteenth-century revivals, the "Jesus people" were of the "counter-culture," "hippie" world that confronted America and the world in the sixties, definitely a clash of cultures. The difference in music being created, a Christian rock and roll (though quite tamed by folk and country music) was in stark contrast with the traditional hymns of the church. Despite the desire for unity ("long hair, short hair, some coats and ties, people finally coming alive . . . ," we sang.) cultures clashed; churches split. Where is the vicarious humanity of Christ, solidarity and substitution, then, in a theology of worship?

How does the double movement of the incarnation relate to worship? This is excluded if worship is defined as only what we do in response to God. James Torrance advocates a different theology of worship that is trinitarian and incarnational, reflecting the double movement of the incarnation: worship is a participation in the worship of the Son to the Father in the Spirit.[35] Instead of a novel theological invention, it is remarkable to see how the double-movement is imbedded almost subconsciously in the great liturgical tradition of the church. An early expression is found in Justin Martyr's *First Apology* from the middle of the second century.[36] The downward

---

34. See Eskridge, *God's Forever Family: The Jesus Movement in America*.

35. James B. Torrance, *Worship, Community, and the Triune God of Grace*.

36. Justin Martyr, *First Apology*, chap. 67, in Richardson, ed., *Early Christian Fathers*, 287–88: "And on the day called Sunday there is a meeting in one place of those who live in cities or the country, and the memoirs of the apostles or the writings of the prophets are read as long as time permits. When the reader has finished, the president in a discourse urges and invites [us] to the imitation of nobler things. Then we all stand up together and offer prayers. And, as said before, when we have finished the prayer, bread is brought, and wine and water, and the president similarly sends up prayers and thanksgivings to the

movement is reflected in the Ministry of the Word. The upward movement to God is reflected in what is called the Ministry of the Faithful (Orthodox), the response to God in prayer, offering, and communion (Reformed), or the Ministry of the Sacrament (Lutheran). What is less clear in all traditions is the place of Jesus Christ our High Priest in leading us in worship (Heb. 8:1), so that often our worship concentrates solely on the deity of Christ (the Ministry of the Word) and easily bypasses the humanity of Christ. Jesus Christ, "the perfect Eucharistic Being," who brings our thanksgiving to the Father along with his (see Matt 11:25 and Luke 10:21 . . . "I thank you, Father, Lord of heaven and earth . . ."). Our responses easily become only cultural without participation in the vicarious *worship* of Christ. With this christological center, perhaps we can have more freedom to accept a diversity of cultural expressions that may not necessarily be our own. Cultures should speak of creativity and freedom without an imperialistic intolerance for the other. Substitution without solidarity breeds intolerance.

Culture involves both that which is determined and that which is chosen. Both carry their own burdens. The vicarious culture of Christ finds us "weary" in our cultured identities, carrying "heavy burdens," and calls us to come to him and find rest in taking upon *his* yoke, his culture in solidarity with ours, yet simultaneously taking our place as substitute (Matt 11:28-30). Jesus actually does and continues to trust, worship, and serve for us and in our place. Therefore we must constantly turn to the biblical testimony about Christ's faith, worship, service, and prayer as a critique and ask ourselves if the church is faithfully joining in that one continuing ministry and life through the Spirit. In Barth's words, is our willing "a participation of man in the being and life of God, a willing of what He wills and a doing of what He does"?[37] We may be, in Clifford Geertz's words, "incomplete or unfinished animals who complete or finish ourselves through culture," yet very well finish ourselves off through cultural genocide if left to our own devices.[38] It is troubling, therefore, when one encounters various forms of synergism in the church, that belief in salvation as fifty percent of God and fifty percent of our response, with Christ as merely the instrument that enables us to respond. So we worship the Father, writes William Dyr-

---

best of his ability, and the congregation assents, saying the Amen: the distribution, and reception of the consecrated [elements] by each one, takes place and they are sent to the absent by the deacons." Cf. Webber, *Worship: Old and New*, 54.

37. Barth, *CD* IV/1: 113. Cf. Dyrness, *The Earth is the Lord's*, 174 n. 30.
38. Geertz, *Interpretation of Culture*, 49. Cf. Dyrness, *The Earth is the Lord's*, 69-70.

ness, "through the work of the Son."[39] Such a view of the atonement sees the Son's work in an only *instrumental* way, as only paying the penalty for our sin, but falls far short of the richness of Christ's vicarious life, death, and resurrection that we see portrayed in the Gospels. Christ is not just the *instrument,* but the *substance* of the atonement. Without him as the active, personal agent, we are still left with the "heavy burdens."

The vicarious humanity of Christ is fulfilled in that upward movement towards God, a movement of joy, the joy of Jesus in the midst of the despair of cultural conflict. The often heavy burden of prayer has been replaced by the vicarious prayers of the Son. The resurrection of Jesus means that help is already here; a witness has already been made within culture as both an affirmation and a critique. Such help is neither remote from nor natural to humanity: it comes into humanity (downward), deep into our actual humanity, in order to recreate humanity in the image of God's Son (upward). The incarnation signifies dying and rising with Christ, the double movement culminating in the vicarious humanity of Christ that descends deeply into human culture in order to recreate a new culture, the vicarious *culture* of Christ, conformed to his perfect faith, worship, and service, his relationship with the Father in the Spirit. Finally it is *his* culture that brings peace and reconciliation, joy in the midst of despair, which my great-grandmother, along with many other immigrants, sought as they encountered a new culture.[40]

---

39. Dyrness, *The Earth is the Lord's*, 74.

40. An earlier version of this essay was presented at the Global Christianity conference, Baylor University, 2005.

CHAPTER THREE

The Vicarious Beauty of Christ and the Aesthetics of the Atonement

AESTHETICS HAUNTS CHRISTIAN THEOLOGY. It both promises and troubles. The psalmist asks "one thing . . . to behold the beauty of the Lord" (Ps 27:4). Yet Yahweh chastises Jerusalem for trusting in their "beauty" by playing the whore (Ezek 16:15). Our age is a sensate age, drunk with images, feelings, and passions. Evangelical churches rush to create more relevant worship services through both the use of incense and video projection of the latest movies. But beauty deceives, laments the weary middle-aged rocker Bob Dylan, agreeing with Plato, at least in theory. We embrace and inundate ourselves with beauty but admit, with the denouement of *King Kong*, it wasn't the airplanes that killed him; it was "beauty that killed the beast."[1]

Atonement does not readily come to mind in discussion of theological aesthetics. What would be its implications if it did? Scottish theologian T. F. Torrance suggests an approach to atonement beyond the recitation of myriad atonement "theories." While it has been common to speak of the atonement as the vicarious death of Christ, Torrance argues that the entirety of Christ's life, death, and resurrection is atoning, lived for our sake and on our behalf. Can we speak of the vicarious *humanity* of Christ? If Christ's life as well as his death is atoning, can we then understand his life as a life of *beauty*, yet also as a *vicarious* life, a life we have been unable to live? Christ, "the perfect Eucharistic being," in Alexander Schmemann's words, lives a life of thanksgiving, faith, obedience, worship, and service

---

1. *King Kong*, directed by Merian C. Cooper and Ernest C. Schoedsack.

that becomes the basis for our lives.² If Christ is beautiful, and if he has his own visions of beauty, does he then establish a critique of our ideas of beauty and aesthetics? What are the implications of the vicarious beauty of Christ for the beauty of God, creation, and redemption, and even for the unity of the true, the beautiful, and the good?

Christ Sees and Is Seen, Hears and Is Heard

Christ is the Word of God indeed, but he is the Word who was heard, seen, and touched according to 1 John (1:1), and whose "glory" was beheld, according to John's Gospel (1:14). He is the Word, the expression of God, the Word that comes from outside, from above. This is the movement from God to humanity. But he is also the response in his faithful humanity, a response that is beautiful because of his harmony with the Father. This is the movement from humanity to God. Both are essential in our understanding of the atonement. A purely humanward movement may indeed demonstrate God's power, yet without the perfect response, humanity is left with only forgiveness of sins and its own resources in order to respond (see figure 1).³

God

Christ the Word of God ↓ ↑ The Vicarious Humanity of Christ

Humanity

Figure 1: The Incarnation

Christ is the one who is not only beheld but also perfectly beholds. The long tradition of Christian portrayals of Christ in art, particularly in iconography, can produce a one-sided emphasis on Christ as one who we see, but who does not see himself. If the one who is pure in heart sees God (Matt 5:8) then the fulfillment the beatific vision so longed for in theological aesthetics is fulfilled first of all in Christ. He is the only one who sees God. We can only see God through him, just as we can only hear the Word of God through him. The Reformed tradition has rightly emphasized the importance of the Word from outside of humanity (despite the "hatred" of

---

2. Schmemann, *For the Life of the World*, 38.
3. Adapted from diagrams by Ray S. Anderson, "A Theology for Ministry," 11, and James B. Torrance, *Worship, Community, and the Triune God of Grace*, 30.

the Word in postmodern culture). However, the incarnation is not only a word from above but also a response from below, the faithful and obedient response of the Son to the Father, a response that is essentially a vision of God. We can think of the baptism of Jesus in Matt 3:16–17: "he *saw* the Spirit of God descending . . . And a *voice* from heaven said, 'This is my Son, the Beloved.'" An act of obedience to the Father, in Jesus' baptism there is both visual and audial in this commissioning of his ministry, a baptism that is vicarious, on behalf of others, a *vicarious repentance*, if you will.[4] Here we have one dramatic manifestation of the vicarious humanity of Christ in an aesthetic moment. The early Christian writing *The Odes of Solomon* presents Christ as actively speaking, and even singing (31:3). This is not too distant from Dietrich Bonhoeffer's suggestion to sing the psalms as continually prayed by Christ.[5]

Christ as seeing, speaking, praying, and singing is not foreign to Karl Barth's insight that to say, "Jesus lives . . . is at once the simplest and the most difficult christological statement."[6] Barth expounds the prophetic office of Christ, "the true witness" as an active Subject, one who lives, not just who *has* lived.[7] "The Glory of the Mediator" for Barth, in this section of the *Church Dogmatics* is that Christ is "the Light of Life." Christ's glory is an aesthetic reality, a light filled with splendor that enlightens our light (Ps 36:9). Beauty brings *delight* and the delight of the Son is in the revelation of the Father: "Jesus *rejoiced* in the Holy Spirit and said, 'I thank you, Father, Lord of heaven and earth, because you have hidden these things from the wise and the intelligent and have revealed them to infants." (Luke 10:21).

Christ as seen and seeing, hearing and being heard provides a wholeness of sight and hearing, as Hans Urs von Balthasar stresses (despite his unfortunate priority of sight over hearing).[8] The form of Christ's beauty, "Christian optics," in David Bentley Hart's words, is a way of seeing God, the world, and the self in a new way.[9] No dualism between creation and redemption can then be accepted. Not only does Christ instate a new

---

4. See Kettler, "The Vicarious Repentance of Christ in the Theology of John McLeod and R.C. Moberly," 529–43; Kettler, *The Vicarious Humanity of Christ and the Reality of Salvation*, 187–204.

5. Bonhoeffer, *Life Together/Prayerbook of the Bible*, 166.

6. Barth, *CD IV*/3.1: 39.

7. Ibid., 44.

8. von Balthasar, *The Glory of the Lord*, Vol. 1, 119–20.

9. Hart, *The Beauty of the Infinite*, 337.

order of seeing (which is Hart's point), but he is also the one who continues to see.[10]

Atonement is the Beauty of Solidarity and Substitution

The vicarious humanity of Christ speaks of the wholeness, the beauty of the life, death, and resurrection of Christ. This harmony is initiated by God's solidarity with humanity in the incarnation. Again, the downward movement of solidarity, from God to humanity comes first, succeeded by the upward movement from humanity to God in Christ's vicarious faith and obedience to the Father on our behalf. In this act he becomes our substitute, not only in paying the penalty for sin, but also in the entirety of our humanity. Evangelicalism and pietism have long had a kind of "aesthetic" in the atonement, basing it on the shed "blood" of Christ. But this view ironically limits substitution, and therefore limits the effect of Christ's atoning life, death, and resurrection on our humanity. There is no beauty in the cross by itself.[11] In contrast, the vicarious humanity of Christ is an aesthetic encompassing the entirety of Christ's humanity and our humanity, the "sweet exchange," suggested by the aesthetics of *The Epistle to Diognetus* (second or third century).[12]

Substitution without solidarity denies the implications of the tragic for the atonement. Hart is right to criticize the use of the tragic when it is viewed as the gospel *in toto*.[13] Atonement is not to be restricted to representation - Christ representing us in solidarity with our suffering - a common theme in contemporary soteriology advocated by Jürgen Moltmann and many others. Nevertheless, atonement loses the first step, the movement from God to humanity, if the Word of God does not identify with the flesh of humanity in travail. Solidarity is an imperative because of the desperate situation of the human creature.

Solidarity without substitution, however, is simply empty empathy and not salvation, as Hart reminds us. What is needed is the inclusion of the vicarious faith and obedience of Christ that leads us through the Holy Spirit on the way to *theosis*, the exaltation of human life emphasized

10. Ibid., 343.
11. Viladesau, *Theological Aesthetics*, 191.
12. *The Epistle to Diognetus* in *The Apostolic Fathers*, Vol. 2, 9.
13. Hart, *The Beauty of the Infinite*, 373–76.

by the Greek fathers, the "participation in the divine nature" in 2 Pet 2:4, because, in the "double movement" of Christ's humiliation and exaltation (Phil 2:5–11), the second movement "Godward" is the act of the vicarious humanity of Christ, his perfect faithfulness and obedience on our behalf towards the Father in the Spirit, reflected in "the ministry of the faithful" (Chrysostom's liturgy), particularly in the Eucharist. In this upward movement, the church joins in the continual song of Christ, a richly aesthetic action (see fig 2). Most theological aesthetics will readily begin with the tangibleness of the incarnation, but often ignore the aesthetic of the "Godward" movement.

God
Solidarity ↓ ↑ Substitution
Humanity

Figure 2

The vicarious humanity of Christ, unlike some theories of the atonement, avoids isolating the death of Christ from his life and resurrection. C. S. Lewis speaks of the importance of the artist in enlarging another's vision: "My own eyes are not enough for me, I will see through those of others."[14] There is a *vicarious* act in art and beauty, doing something that we cannot do by ourselves (see fig 3). The beauty of the unity of the vicarious life, death, and resurrection of Christ, enters the totality of our experience, including the death on Holy Saturday as advocated by Hans Urs von Balthasar and Alan Lewis, despite the criticism of David Bentley Hart that this is another example of "tragic" theology.[15] The vicarious humanity of Christ does not ignore tragedy at the expense of victory (atonement is both solidarity and substitution) because it is realistic about our desperate plight.

God
The Beauty of God Revealed ↓ ↑ The Vicarious Beauty of Christ
Humanity

Figure 3

14. C. S. Lewis, *An Experiment in Criticism*, 140.
15. von Balthasar, *Mysterium Paschale*, Alan E. Lewis, *Between Cross and Resurrection*, 44, and Hart, *The Beauty of the Infinite*, 373.

The totality and comprehensiveness of the human situation demonstrates the judgment of beauty. "You cannot see my face," Yahweh pronounces to Moses, "for no one shall see me and live" (Exod 33:20). It is Christ who removes the veil of Moses (2 Cor 3:12–18). The spiritual blindness of humanity is particularly emphasized by Jesus in his controversies with the Pharisees and as a critique of unbelief. They are "blind guides of the blind" (Matt 15:14). They see but do not perceive (Matt 13:14). "Do you have eyes and fail to see?" Jesus asks his disciples (Mark 8:18). In effect, he is asking, Are we to limit the beautiful to what we perceive beauty to be?[16] We need to remember that the Fall was precipitated by an object that was "a delight to the eyes" (Gen 3:6). Tragedy or human need correspond well to the preoccupation of modern art with despair. If the tragic is but part of the first movement of the atonement, from God to humanity, then despair should not be ruled out in a Christian appreciation of art. The lament psalms are brought to dramatic climax in the cry of abandonment on the cross (Matt 27:46). Atonement may be more than this, but it is not less. The vicarious humanity of Christ guarantees a second movement as well: from humanity to God, from the Son to the Father, a movement of victory and joy, joy that comes out from despair but does not avoid it.

The problems of aesthetics are many, both philosophical and practical. The vicarious beauty of Christ provides a possible different way of considering the puzzle of what is true beauty and what is genuine art, as well as a critique of the failure of the church to develop a robust theological aesthetic. If the true, the beautiful, and the good have been united in the vicarious beauty of Christ, then the traditional burdens in aesthetics of Aristotelian knowledge (a supreme confidence that we can know objective beauty) or Nietzschean power (the creative act as self-worship) are relativized by Christ the vicarious Artist, Musician, Poet, and Dancer. True, some traditions have been tempted to exalt the humanward movement of the spoken Word at the expense of the Godward movement of a sensory response. But a theology of the vicarious beauty of Christ stands against such a one-sided gospel and affirms the beauty of the Son's response as the one who indeed is pure in heart and therefore sees and hears God for us and in our place.

---

16. Dyrness, *Visual Faith*, 75.

The "Wholly Other" Beauty of Christ

The one who is pure in heart, however, who possesses the vision of God, is not beautiful as we would expect: "He has not the form or majesty that we should look at him, nothing in his appearance that we should desire him" (Isa 53:2). Or listen to Bernard of Clairvaux: "How beautiful you are to me, my Lord, even in the very discarding of your beauty!"[17] Such a view of beauty may take us far from the ideal of Plato or the symmetry of Aristotle. Sentimentality in religious art is also roundly criticized for promoting an innocuous, placid Jesus, for example. Yet it is equally problematic to portray a Jesus as nothing but pain, perhaps implying a view of atonement virtually separating the wrathful Father from the innocent Son. Criticisms of Mel Gibson's film on Jesus come to mind. The grotesque may lead us to grace (see Flannery O'Connor's fiction), but it must not be glorified in itself. Mother Teresa saw the beauty of Christ in the sick and unattractive of the world, and thus was able to minister to them: "Though you hide yourself behind the unattractive disguise of the irritable, the exacting, the unreasonable, may I still recognize you, and say: 'Jesus, my patient, how sweet it is to see you.'"[18]

Our sentiments about what is beautiful and what is art are certainly culturally and psychologically relative. This is not surprising to the vicarious beauty of Christ, which comes with its own definition of what beauty is, in the form of the Suffering Servant, as one example. Barth's criticism of religion can also be transferred to a criticism of our ideas of beauty: Like our preconceived ideas of religion, our preconceived ideas of beauty must be displaced and replaced by Christ.[19] In no other place is there such a bounty of beauty. Despite our love for creaturely beauty, that creaturely beauty inspires us to search for *a beauty we have never experienced,* C. S. Lewis reminds us.[20] This is a "wisdom" hidden for ages, "for our glory" that the rulers of this age did not understand, "for if they had, they would not have crucified the Lord of *glory* (beauty!) (1 Cor 2:7–8). Is this not the "wholly other" beauty of Christ? The form of Christ brings its own beauty not by thoughts or words about beauty but by this beauty itself. The form of Christ is his splendor, a unity between beauty and being, in von Balthasar's

---

17. Bernard of Clairvaux, *On the Song of Songs II*, 239.
18. Mother Teresa quoted in Muggeridge, *Something Beautiful for God*, 75.
19. Barth, *CD* I/2, "The Revelation of God as the Abolition of Religion," 280–361.
20. C. S. Lewis, "The Weight of Glory," 4.

words.[21] The beauty of God takes the place of our ideas of beauty. But does this mean that there is no analogy of being between Christ's beauty and the beauty of this world, between uncreated Beauty and created beauty, or Christ's response to God and the need for our response?

The Vicarious Knowledge of Beauty

Is the analogy of being *(analogia entis)*, famously denounced by Karl Barth as the Roman Catholic teaching that was "the invention of the antichrist," and recently resurrected by the Orthodox theologian David Bentley Hart, really the best language to express the relationship between uncreated Beauty and created beauty, between and God and his creation?[22] The admirable intention of the *analogia's* followers is to maintain a continuity between God, the source of all being and being itself, and therefore, God and creation. Hart criticizes Barth's "radical rupture" between the two.[23] But if Christ is the vicarious beauty that takes the place of our preconceived ideas of beauty, then does not this vicarious, substitutionary reality better address the radical nature of our problem and provide the equally radical solution? Is Christ's beauty first of all a *vicarious, not analogous, knowledge?*

True, God as the source of all can be said to overflow in sharing being with others (Pseudo-Dionysius). God may seem more "available" in an analogy of being, but at what price? According to Alexander Schmemann, the analogy of being (as well as his critique of "Barthianism") fails to relate the natural and the supernatural, thereby encouraging secularization.[24] The supernatural will eventually collapse into the natural. Is there a better way?

Atonement involves both solidarity and substitution. This is claimed by the vicarious humanity of Christ. In terms of theological epistemology, this double movement partakes of our language yet immediately gives it new meaning. It may have analogous elements (solidarity with our humanity), but ultimately this is a part of the vicarious language of the Word made flesh. Should this not be true in terms of beauty?

---

21. von Balthasar, *The Glory of the Lord*, Vol. 1, 119. See also Dyrness, *Visual Faith*, 90.
22. Barth, *CD* I/1, second edition: xiii.
23. Hart, *The Beauty of the Infinite*, 408.
24. Schmemann, *For the Life of the World*, 129.

The judgment of the vicarious humanity of Christ is that Christ takes our place at every point. Our need is that total. The "radical rupture" in salvation history that Hart criticizes is a result of our radical need. The need made manifest by the vicarious humanity is not, however, in contrast to some Protestant views, predicated upon the depth of the Fall but on the aesthetic riches of his excellency (Jonathan Edwards), a harmony between the Father and the Son revealed in the incarnation, that is, in the vicarious beauty of Christ.[25]

The biblical exhortation to walk by faith and not by sight and the description of faith as the conviction of things not seen (2 Cor 5:7; Heb 11:1) does not have to be embarrassing to theological aesthetics, for a subset of the vicarious humanity of Christ is his vicarious faith. The faith of Jesus is vicarious, replacing and establishing our faith so that our sight does not become detrimental to faith, so that our perception of beauty as only physical (whether we think of Brad Pitt and Angelina Jolie, or Cary Grant and Ingrid Bergman) does not deceive. Faith becomes irrelevant if our being and God's being are not distinguished. Unlike with us, in Christ, faith and sight are in a beautiful harmony. We need his ears and his eyes. Our response is made possible by his response. In this way we are to share in his "glory" (John 17:22).

Jesus' faith is in God the Father (see the Lord's Prayer). His glory is that of "a father's only son" (John 1:14). God is Father for Jesus. However, Jesus names God as his Father according to his own definition.[26] If the language of analogy is to be used, the analogy of relations, as suggested by Barth and Bonhoeffer, seems preferable, for language of God as Father is personal and relational.[27] The Son gives definition to what it means for God to be Father, not our preconceived ideas or experiences. Otherwise, we are hopelessly projecting our experiences upon God. Grace is a personal and relational reality.[28] Beauty can also become impersonal if it is simply related to the commonality of being. The vicarious act of the Son is a personal action, motivated by unconditional love. In fact, is the beauty of Christ any more majestic, any more a reflection of the triune life, than in his relations with the Father and with humanity (Gal 4:4–5)?

---

25. See Mitchell, *Jonathan Edwards on the Experience of Beauty*, 4–7, 35–38.
26. James B. Torrance, *Worship, Community, and the Triune God of Grace*, 123.
27. Bonhoeffer, *Creation and Fall*, 65, and Barth, *CD* III/1: 228–30 and III/2: 220–21.
28. Begbie, *Voicing Creation's Praise*, 145–48. See also Dyrness, *Visual Faith*, 97.

The personal action of the movement of the Son to the Father in the Spirit is a movement of harmonious beauty that we cannot make, a knowledge of God that is an event, not a principle nor a doctrine. This beautified event is Christ as the Light of life, in whose light we see light (John 1:4; Ps 36:9). As in the Nicene Creed, Christ is "Light from Light," the Giver of grace who is the Gift of grace (T. F. Torrance).[29] The present life of the resurrected, ascended Jesus is also a profound testament to Christ as the Light by whom *vicariously* we see light, by which we can see in a new and wonderful way creation as God intended, the beauty of the Light of life in Christ that can only be given to us.[30]

The Vicarious Beauty of Christ and Creation, Old and New

The aesthetics of the atonement involve the recreation, the redemption of that which was broken, the reconciliation of God, humanity, and the cosmos into a new harmony. We behold the glory of Christ, Christ seeing and being seen, hearing and being heard.

However, our notions of beauty can be notoriously limited. The contemporary (though hardly novel) obsession over physical beauty is a problem of the isolation of physical beauty from a wider and deeper purpose, (see David and Bathsheba in 2 Sam 11:2).[31] Barth is right that, frankly, we perceive ourselves as primarily sensual.[32] Yet Jesus has eyes that are far superior to the powers of my other "heroes": Superman's X-ray vision or the ability of the Shadow to know what lurks in the hearts of men. The Fourth Gospel tells of Jesus' refusal to entrust himself to those who believed because of the signs, "for he himself knew what was in everyone" (John 2:24–25). On the positive side, Nathanael is amazed that Jesus knows him as "an Israelite in whom there is no deceit" (John 1:48). "Where did you get to know me?" he asks. Indeed, Jesus also sees beauty beyond simply the physical.

The high priesthood of Christ (Heb 8:1) and the church as the "royal priesthood" (1 Pet. 3:9; Rev 1:9), however, proclaim the giftedness of creation as its beauty, which includes physical beauty (see *The Song of Solomon*

---

29. T. F. Torrance, *The Trinitarian Faith*, 138.
30. Barth, *CD* II/1: 665.
31. Dyrness, *Visual Faith*, 82.
32. Barth, *CD* III/2: 91.

and *Revelation*). Simone Weil famously teaches that beauty may be the only way that we can allow God to penetrate us, yet adds the caveat, "*If it were made true and pure*, it would sweep all secular life in a body to the feet of God."[33] Weil reflects a "a natural inclination to love beauty" in much the same way the Neoplatonic philosophical tradition presents creation as the first step in ascent to God (Plotinus, Gregory of Nyssa). Yet are these inclinations necessary if Christ sees creation in all of its splendor for us with the eyes of his faith? In fact, is there not the necessity for his vision of creation? The physical world is not only benign; it can be diseased and chaotic as well. Christ prays the psalm of the heavens declaring the glory of God (Ps 19:1) when it is difficult, if not impossible for us to do so in a world that we see of the transitory, the random, and the absurd. The atonement is by grace alone, as creation is out of nothing, by grace alone.

The psalmist sees "the beauty of the Lord" in "the house of the Lord," in the context of worship (Ps 27:4). In terms of worship, perhaps the category of witness can be applied to the icon as well as it is done to Holy Scripture, for example, by the theology of Karl Barth. The Fourth General Council of Constantinople (869–870), in its response to the iconoclasm controversy, argued that icons are to be given the same honor as "the book of the Holy Gospels."[34] At this point, all Christian worship, simple or ornate, can see the arts in worship as a witness to Jesus Christ, or even as participating in Christ, in his vicarious humanity, bearing witness to God (see Christ as "The True Witness" in Barth).[35]

This is a witness that unites the beautiful with the true, in terms of knowledge of God, but also unites the beautiful with the good by seeing a beauty in the rejected, the ugly, and the grotesque of society. The beauty of Christ ignites a compassion for those of little account in society, including the fallen, the poor, children, and the elderly.

The theology of the atonement often suffers when both aspects of the double movement of the incarnation have not been recognized: the humanward act of descent in solidarity with humanity and the Godward act of ascent in substitution for humanity by the vicarious humanity, even beauty, of Christ. Christ's beauty is an atoning response as well as a contemplation of God. Karl Barth speaks of his renowned love for the music of Mozart

---

33. Weil, *Waiting for God*, 102–03 (emphasis mine).

34. The Fourth General Council of Constantinople cited in Thiessen, *Theological Aesthetics*, 65.

35. Barth, *CD* IV/3.1: 368–434.

not in terms of the humanward movement of the Word, but the Godward movement of faith, obedience, and worship: "Mozart does not wish to say anything: he just sings and sounds."[36] Is this not a reflection of the act of the vicarious beauty of Christ, an atoning response in his life, death, and resurrection, a beauty found in his perfect relationship of harmony with the Father in the Spirit?

In the end, beauty appears to be gratuitous in the same way that grace is.[37] And so one can respond either with gratefulness or with indifference. His glory was "full of grace and truth," yet "the world did not know him" (John 1:14, 10). The vicarious beauty of Christ is his continuing response to the Father, a place for grace to ascend as well as descend, in continuing worship and obedience. This is a beautiful response that humanity can join in together with Christ through the Holy Spirit. Christ, like art and beauty, is revealed by grace. Art and beauty, as Dostoevsky claims, meet a hunger that we accept unconditionally.[38] This is grace recognized and received: "But to all who received him, who believed in his name, he gave power to become children of God" (John 1:12). *Theosis* will one day be completed, for "when he is revealed, we will be like him, for we will see him as he is" (1 John 3:2), that is, when we fully share in the vision and hearing of Christ.[39]

---

36. Barth, *Wolfgang Amadeus Mozart*, 37.
37. Hart, *The Beauty of the Infinite*, 438.
38. Dostoevsky cited in Kjetsaa, *Fyodor Dostoevsky*, 139.
39. An earlier version of this essay was presented at the Christian Systematic Theology section, American Academy of Religion annual meeting, 2005.

CHAPTER FOUR

God's Joy in Action

*Creation Out of Nothing and the
Vicarious Humanity of Christ*

PROMINENT IN THE THEOLOGICAL heritage of Thomas F. Torrance is his distinctive advocacy of two doctrines: creation out of nothing (*creatio ex nihilo*) and the vicarious humanity of Christ. The thesis of this essay is that the relationship between these two doctrines has great implications for the pastoral and practical problem of how one finds joy in the midst of despair. Creation out of nothing emphasizes an act of God that is a truly free act, ruling out any necessity or compulsion. Creation, thus, is an expression of God's covenant love. The vicarious humanity of Christ, likewise, teaches that God acts out of the nothing of the "barrenness" of Sarah, the inability of human being to respond with perfect faith, obedience, service, and worship to the Father. Jesus Christ, in the power of the Holy Spirit, has done this, on our behalf and in our place. This act includes a genuine joy from Jesus in the midst of the despair of this world (Luke 10:21; Heb 12:2) in which we may now participate. God rejoices in both creation and redemption when we are unable to do so in the marriage of *creatio ex nihilo* and the vicarious humanity of Christ. Thus, the relationship yet distinction between God and creation is maintained (versus some tendencies in David Bentley Hart). A theological anthropology is also grounded in the vicarious joy of Christ, not a capacity within human beings nor in popular attempts to base humanity in a "purpose driven life."

In the spring of 1981, I was fortunate to be the teaching assistant to Thomas F. Torrance during his visit to Fuller Theological Seminary in Pasadena, California. I had some familiarity with Dr. Torrance's work, being a student of Ray Anderson's, a former student of Torrance's. But I was not prepared for what became a life-changing event. For a solid month, I escorted Dr. Torrance around Fuller and southern California as he lectured on theology, science, the Nicene Creed, as well as even encountering a homeless person! Even nearing seventy, Dr. Torrance was a veritable whirlwind of theological wrestling and evangelical conviction. As reflected in the gospel that he preached, Torrance exhibited both the mercy and righteousness, both the grace and holiness of God, always with a kind of impish wit that many found endearing, and some, convicting. When once a disheveled homeless person meandered into the Fuller cafeteria for breakfast, seeking for the usual patronizing attitude he received from seminarians, this time he sat at table with Tom Torrance and myself. After hearing some pseudo-religious mumbo-jumbo, Torrance looked at him with compassion and simply said, "My dear fellow, I think you need to be born again." Tom Torrance was known for his frankness, of course, which many respected and others criticized. Above all, Torrance liked to see himself always as a missionary, like his father, but one to theologians and scientists. I was privileged to see and hear that missionary in action with a kind of joy that lifted many of us typical seminary students at Fuller out of our personal despairs into the joy of Jesus, a joy that brought genuine healing. I still hear from friends of that time and how important Dr. Torrance was for them personally as well as theologically.

I was never an enthusiast for science in my schooldays. As a seminary student I was concerned about apologetics, the defense of the faith, but was radically challenged by Karl Barth that the best apologetics is a good dogmatics! Ray Anderson's pioneering work in integrating theology and ministry while being influenced by Barth and Torrance became extremely important to me. But T. F. Torrance's lectures on the Nicene Creed and science made me become aware of the need for a trinitarian, Christocentric theology that is engaged with the world; a theology of redemption and reconciliation should not be separated from a doctrine of creation. Torrance's doctrine of the vicarious humanity of Christ led me to write my Ph.D. dissertation that was published as *The Vicarious Humanity of Christ and the Reality of Salvation* (1991), a critique of contemporary soteriologies based on the vicarious humanity of Christ. Other articles have followed developing the further implications of the vicarious humanity of Christ, as well as the book, *The God Who Believes: Faith, Doubt, and the Vicarious Humanity of Christ* (2005) and a volume entitled, *The God Who Rejoices: Joy, Despair, and the Vicarious Humanity of Christ* (2010). This essay takes the agenda of the latter one step further. Taking Torrance's concern for science and a doctrine of creation, and seeing *creatio ex nihilo* in the context of the vicarious humanity, in light of the question of how one can find joy in the midst of despair, is the agenda for this essay. It is my meager way to pay tribute to, but also the further explore critically and theologically, the theology and ministry of Thomas F. Torrance.

Joy and despair are very creaturely experiences. Human, yes, but first of all, creaturely. Are there any implications of Christ's vicarious joy (Luke 10:21; Heb 12:2) in the midst of despair for our response to creation as a whole? And then, how would that influence our attitude to the very practical and pastoral problem of how one finds joy in the midst of the despair of life?

Creation is one of the cardinal Christian doctrines. In contemporary Kansas, however, hearing the word "creation" immediately brings in "evolution." Among theologians, beyond concerns to relate creation to modern science, issues such as *creatio ex nihilo* (creation out of nothing) are discussed, with the old and the new joined in a basic question about how God is related to the world: as distinct (traditional theism), as identical (pantheism), or as part of (panentheism).

Creation Out of Nothing:
God's Life Gives Life

Created life does not generate itself. It is beholden to the One who is Life in himself (regardless of the means, natural or supernatural). Humanity is first of all a creature that receives: "then the Lord God formed man from the dust of the ground, and breathed into his nostrils the breath of life; and the man became a living being" (Gen 2:7). God, the source of life, bestows upon humanity their breath. The very breath of life is something that is given and therefore can only be received. To receive, therefore, is at the essence of creatureliness and humanity, just as the Son receives from the Father. "God's breath gives to the man formed of dust that which he does not possess and cannot give himself as such."[1] At the beginning of creation God is involved in a vicarious act—doing what we cannot do for ourselves—in bestowing upon us the very breath of life. We should not limit the vicarious work of God to salvation alone. As Jesus the Vicarious

---

1. Barth, *CD* III/1: 245.

One is "the true witness" (Barth, CD, IV/3.1), humanity in its creation becomes the vicarious human being that bears witness to God, giving voice to mute creation.[2] Barth cites Michelangelo's ability to portray this so very well in his portrait of the breath of life being breathed into Adam. Yet this free gift can always be withdrawn, as we see in the history of the judgment upon Israel.[3] The only hope of all humanity in judgment is the One who on the cross cried out, "Father, into your hands I commit my spirit" (Luke 23:46). His obedient spirit (breath) was given back to God. Even in the utmost extreme of estrangement from the Father, Jesus lives vicariously in giving back our rebellious spirits to God. So that Stephen, at the point of his martyrdom, will imitate his Lord by crying out, "Lord Jesus, receive my spirit" (Acts 7:59). He prays to Jesus because he is the mediator, not simply because he is God, as in so much contemporary worship that deemphasizes the mediatory worship by Jesus to the Father. It is curious in Barth, however, that although he rightly sees the Spirit as address and gift, he does not emphasize the humanity of Jesus as the one who receives the address and gift: "The spirit, then, continues beyond death, not as something belonging to man, but as the divine address and gift to man, which remains in readiness for him . . ."[4]

God has his own life. As the uncreated life, he is able to create life. He knows what life is all about. As Barth comments, the tension between science and theology could have been avoided to some extent if theology was more confident concerning what it believes about God. Out of that belief, then comes the doctrine of creation. That belief in God made known through God's self-revelation reveals that we should be more certain about knowledge of God than we are about the creature![5] The knowledge of God we have through Jesus Christ (and this immediately raises the distinctiveness of Christology for the doctrine of creation) is knowledge of the God who is Trinity. The desperate attempts, therefore, of many to find the analogy between creation and the human creature, are not as promising as the analogy between creation and "the eternal begetting of the Son by the Father," in "the inner life of God Himself."[6] This is no lonely God who

---

2. Ibid., 247.
3. Ibid., 247–48.
4. Ibid., 249.
5. Ibid., 6.
6. Ibid., 13–14.

is forced to create out of need, as the "let us" of Genesis 1 reminds us.[7] He is the free God who is free to create as a demonstration of his deity, yet to create as a correspondence to his inner life as Father, Son, and Spirit, a life lived in belonging and relationship.[8] God is free to do something new: to become a creator. T. F. Torrance further suggests that the Fathers advocated *creatio ex nihilo*, creation out of nothing, because of the stupendous effect of God raising Jesus from the dead, demonstrating "the absolute power of God over life and death, over all being and non-being."[9] The very nature of biblical faith, Paul contends, is expressed in Abraham's faith in analogy with creation, faith in the God "who gives life to the dead and calls into existence the things that do not exist" (Rom 4:17).[10] Hebrews 11:3 confirms this relationship between creation out of nothing, faith, and resurrection: "By faith we understand that the worlds were prepared by the word of God, so that what is seen was made from things that are not visible." It is nothing but the invisible word of God that is the source of creation, but we can only know this by faith.[11] Creation is accessible to us, but the God believed in as creator is not. God the creator is an object of faith and why the Creed does not speak of believing in heaven and earth but in God, "the maker of heaven and earth."

Creation and Covenant

All of this is to say that the Bible is grace from beginning to end, one covenant of grace in which Jesus Christ is always present, including creation.[12] He is in fact the goal of creation: The "mystery" of God's will has become known "in Christ, as a plan for the fullness of time, to gather up all things in him, things in heaven and things on earth" (Eph 1:10). As Irenaeus taught against the Gnostics in the second century, the Creator and the Deliverer are the same. Therefore, as Barth points out, history is not to be understood from my standpoint, "but that my own standpoint, my existence, has been

---

7. Ibid., 183.

8. Barth, *Dogmatics in Outline*, 52: Barth, *CD*, III/1:13; T. F. Torrance, *The Trinitarian Faith*, 93.

9. T. F. Torrance, *The Trinitarian Faith*, 97.

10. Barth, *CD*, III/2: 153.

11. Barth, *Dogmatics in Outline*, 52.

12. Barth, *CD* III/1: 44–45.

given to me by the One who in this history has already dealt with me . . ."[13] Since God has delivered me, as the people of the exodus knew, I now know God the creator.[14] As Barth confesses, "I always come from God the Creator when I am confronted by God the Deliverer."[15]

The basis of creation is covenant, the covenant, the pledge that God unconditionally and unilaterally makes to creation. We cannot know that by our perceptions of whole towns like Greensburg, Kansas, a town of 1,500 people wiped off the map in less than an hour by a tornado in the spring of 2007. Did God love Greensburg? Not by our perceptions. That is not how I would treat a loved one. But the meaning of the covenant of grace reveals the meaning of creation that is hidden from us. That is why it is so important for Barth as a part of his critique of natural theology to stress that creation is not the covenant.[16] Natural theology dies of suffocation at the hands of innocent suffering and evil. But the love that the Father has for the Son, and the love that the Son on the cross is able to have for the Father, means that the fate of creation is in the hands of the covenant of grace, not the chaos and randomness of tornadoes and their tragedies. "The existence and being of the one loved are not identical with the fact that it is loved."[17] Much pastoral sensitivity, empathy, and feeling must be used to coax the comfort out of this statement of Barth's, but I believe it can and should be done. For Barth continues: "This can be said only in respect of the love with which God loves Himself—the Father the Son and the Son the Father in the Holy Spirit." And the love that the Father has for the Son, and that the Son vicariously knows that he is loved, for our sake, is the center of genuine pastoral counsel. The one covenant of grace is the hermeneutic of creation. Out of the *nihilo* of tragedy and our inability to believe comes the Word of God: "I have said this to you, so that in me you may have peace. In the world you face persecution. But take courage: I have conquered the world!" (John 16:33).

---

13. Ibid., 45.

14. Anderson, *The Soul of Ministry: Forming Leaders for God's People*, 54–59: "The Covenant of God Which Precedes Creation" and Moses as "the first theologian" of *ex nihilo*, 35–42.

15. Barth, *CD* III/1: 45.

16. Ibid., 97.

17. Ibid.

The Vicarious Faith of Christ and the "Barrenness" of Faith

Creation out of nothing and faith are intertwined even more so in the vicarious faith of Christ which exists in the midst of the "barrenness" of our faith, much like Sarah's.[18] "Not man and not a wisdom or folly, a power or impotence, immanent in the world of man, willed and accomplished in the creature, but God—the God who rejoiced in man as in His own image."[19] God is the one who rejoices, therefore we can rejoice. God rejoices in his "pure act of creativity."[20] The *ex nihilo* of creation is the same as the *ex nihilo* of redemption: Both are founded in the faith and obedience of the Son to the Father in the Spirit, a faith and obedience that needs no cooperation from us. Justification by faith rightly recognizes our inability, just as demonstrated in our very creation. Faith is not based on anything that is perceptible but on "the conviction of things not seen" (Heb 11:1), which is where we find so much of our despair, in our perceptions of reality, which may or may not be accurate. Melancholy has been defined as "fear and sadness without cause," but it is more appropriate to add as Joshua Wolf Shenk does in his book on Lincoln's melancholy, "without apparent cause, or disproportionate to apparent cause."[21] Our perceptions, as postmodern critics do not tire of reminding us, are notoriously unreliable, and at least biased. That is why we need the vicarious faith of Christ. We do not have accurate perceptions of God, his nature, or of ourselves, or our pathologies. Our angst and alienation will not be healed by a correct worldview. That is why Paul exhorts his readers to set their minds on Christ, seated at the right hand of God in the heavenlies and seek those things that are above (Col 3:2.). What does Christian existence mean but to build it upon God alone, not on any "worldview" or comprehension of creation, for our lives are "hidden with Christ in God" (Col 3:3).[22]

---

18. Anderson, *The Soul of Ministry*, "The Grace of God Which Presupposes Barrenness," 43–51.
19. Barth, *CD* III/1: 99.
20. Ibid., 100.
21. Shenk, *Lincoln's Melancholy*, 212.
22. Barth, *CD* III/2: 156. On worldview: 6–10, 444–47.

Christ the Mediator of Creation, Old and New

Christian faith is anchored on the revealed Word of God, not on anything in the created world, including a worldview, as attractive as that is to many contemporary Christians. A worldview simply violates the epistemological reality of the resurrection of Jesus from the dead. Jesus' resurrection is not just a continuation but a resurrection. This is also true for the Christian's resurrected destiny: a "new creation." Such a belief can only be based on belief in God and God alone. The foundation for that faith is the faith of Jesus of Nazareth. Although much maligned, this is the significance of the patristic doctrine of *creatio ex nihilo*, creation out of nothing.[23] This means that creation is utterly dependent on nothing less than God's own act, contrasting with Plato's view of creation in the *Timaeus* in which creation develops out of God. Rather, *creatio ex nihilo* is the wonderful proclamation that God, in the fullness of his life, creates something distinct from himself. He does not jealously guard his being. He does not demand that creation be a part of him, as in contemporary trends such as process theology. Barth's words are memorable: "No, what God does not grudge the world is creaturely reality . . ."[24] Creation is to God's glory, David Bentley Hart contends, because it is "needless," love expressed gratuitously, out of nothing.[25]

One wonders, however, if Hart's stress on the analogy of being can avoid a necessary not contingent relationship between God and creation. Hart desperately wants to join God and the world "at the hip," as it were, for understandable reasons. He objects rightly to dualisms from Plato to Bultmann in which a gnostic separation of God from creation is all too evident. If this is so, Hart argues, how can we maintain creation's goodness if there is such a separation from God?[26] His alternative, however, is the tradition of the *logos asarkos*, the Word of God apart from the flesh of Jesus Christ,

---

23. See T. F. Torrance, *The Trinitarian Faith*, 95–98; *The Ground and Grammar of Theology*, 54–74; *God and Rationality*, 39; *The Christian Doctrine of God*, 207–9; *Divine and Contingent Order*, vii, 32; Gunton, "The Doctrine of Creation," 141–42, where he states that the doctrine came about "by virtue of the trinitarian form of the doctrine;" See also Barth, CD, III/1: 16 and Colyer, *How to Read T. F. Torrance*, 168–73 and McGrath, *T. F. Torrance*, 191–92.

24. Barth, *Dogmatics in Outline*, 55.

25. Hart, *The Beauty of the Infinite*, 251.

26. Ibid., 105.

which has a long tradition back to Justin Martyr because of apologetic reasons in a Graeco-Roman culture that thoroughly imbibed *logos* as eternal reason. "The Christian Logos must be conceived of as containing all of creation and history within itself."[27] Unfortunately, the *logos asarkos* easily becomes distinct from Jesus Christ, the incarnate Son of God who became human and dwelt among us, teaching, healing, dying, and rising, but most of all, living the actual life of faith, obedience, worship, and service to the Father in the Spirit that we are unable to live. According to Colin Gunton, Thomas Aquinas, in contrast to John Duns Scotus, had little place for the agency of Christ in creation, reflecting the subsequent Western tradition of a "highly abstract theology of the second person of the Trinity, with the result that the New Testament linking of Jesus Christ and creation ceases to be determinative for the theology of creation."[28] Hart can even say that "the world is comprised by God's being." Hart rightly conceives the Trinity as the eternal source of God's "divine delight" (an aesthetical aspect to the nature of God certainly), and therefore with its own differential, not just a Neoplatonic overflow of being.[29] But does he really want to deny the correspondence of that differential in the act of creation out of nothing? Rather than "another world" Hart would rather speak of the world as "infinitely greater than one might expect."[30] One can agree with his attempt to avoid a dualism such as between the spiritual (or existential) and the physical (as he sees in Bultmann and modern Protestantism), separating faith from the wider reality. But the problem of dualism is not solved by retreating to a kind of monism in which there is no distinction between the spiritual and the physical. Unitary thinking does not deny the different realms of heaven and earth; what it does criticize is not recognizing that in the incarnation there is a genuine communication and intersection. Heaven still remains heaven and earth still remains earth. God is still God and is not to be identified with his creation.

Ray Anderson tells the story of the exasperated parishioner who responded to the young pastor Anderson's theological preaching on the doctrine of God: "If God is omniscient, I can easily assent to the fact that he knows everything. What I want to know is, does he know who I am?"[31]

---

27. Ibid.
28. Gunton, *The Triune Creator*, 120–21.
29. Hart, *The Beauty of the Infinite*, 104.
30. Ibid., 105.
31. Anderson, *The Soul of God*, 20.

It is too easy to discount the comment as simply typical of our narcissistic age: It's all about me. No, the doctrine of God is a pastoral problem. So, as Anderson once said in a lecture, "It is better that God is somewhere than everywhere!" (There was quite a response from the class.) Hart's proclamation that "the world is comprised by God's being" sounds pious but does not possess the gospel proclamation of the eternal Word of God who became flesh and sat at table with men and women, boys and girls. Hart contends that the difference between God and creation is not just "negative," but is "peace and joy," since "the world is comprised of God's being."[32] But is this the joy of Jesus, the joy of the one who lives his life on our behalf and in our place simply out of love and because we need this so desperately? Hart rightly affirms that our relationship to God is "the creation's participation in the being that God gives as his gift."[33] But as gift, this is not something that we know or experience apart from the mediation of Christ, the Word becoming flesh, dying and rising on our behalf and in our place. God gives us our own being as a gift. That is grace at the beginning of creation. There is no inherent tendency toward opposition or rupture because the difference in God and humanity is in correspondence (but not identity) with the distinct difference between the Father and the Son: The Son genuinely has faith in and obeys the Father. Creation's participation in the being of God comes from that gift of the Son's relationship to the Father in the Spirit.

In Hart's theology of the analogous relationship between God and creation, there is a strain in seeking to find the connection between the two; so much so that he ends up speaking of "the love of and desire for God and creation that somehow imitates the way God loves and desires God, and loves and desires creation in God."[34] "Somehow"? The "somehow" exists because Hart has forgotten the absolute necessity of the mediation of Christ, the vicarious priest of creation. It is Christ who gives voice to mute creation in his priestly ministry on behalf of fallen humanity. He is the Word of God in his deity, but he is also the Receiver of the Word in his humanity. Creation comes about by God's address (Gen 1:28), creating "a history of being" for humanity, representing creation.[35] The fullness of this is seen in the address of the incarnate Son by the Father: "And a voice from heaven said, 'This is my Son, the Beloved, with whom I am well pleased'"

---

32. Hart, *The Beauty of the Infinite*, 177.
33. Ibid., 251.
34. Ibid., 307.
35. Anderson, *On Being Human*, 34.

(Matt 3:17). Humanity has been addressed but there has been no response. We need, and the Father needs, the response of Jesus. Anderson puts it succinctly:

> God has differentiated between the creatures and himself through his Word. However, the creatures themselves have no power of differentiation because the Word has not come to them in such a way that their creaturely nature becomes a vehicle for expressing that Word.[36]

Hart, of course, would disagree. The analogy of being guarantees a created correspondence between our being and God's being. But of what use is Christ the mediator then? Can Hart really take seriously the doctrine of *creatio ex nihilo* without avoiding the twin problems, as Anderson suggests, of determinism and perfectionism? Ironically for one otherwise ill-disposed to Reformed theology, would Hart share the temptation toward determinism if, in Anderson's words, the possibilities of creation become "a necessary extension of its own nature" rather than a "new creation" through the power of the Word of God? And can perfectionism be avoided if one can expect creation to naturally realize its potential, albeit aided by Christ? Creation out of nothing, Anderson contends, allows creation to be created good, but not from any Aristotelian realization of the actual from the potential. A "genuine relation" between God and creation is maintained by *creatio ex nihilo* (difficult for pantheism and panentheism), which, we might add, is founded on and then fulfilled by the distinct relation of love, faith, obedience, and service between the Father and the Son in the Spirit, including the Son's continual offering to the Father. "Rahner's rule" is true at this point: The economic Trinity (how God appears to us in the incarnation) is the same as the immanent Trinity (who God is in himself).[37]

God's Freedom to Joyfully Create and Love and the Joyful Response of Jesus

God's ego is not swollen. Simply out of his love and grace, the eternal Word of God brings into being that which did not previously exist. God is free to love. The most obvious testimony to that freedom to love is simply in the fact that we exist, rather than not existing. My despair develops from all

36. Ibid.
37. Rahner, *The Trinity*.

sorts of subsequent events in my history. To be created is who I am, and, first of all, to be created by the free grace and love of God.

Creation, therefore, is an act of joy by God. Despair may come later, but first comes joy, the joy of creativity, of bringing into being that which was previously not. John Macmurray suggests that this is the significance of God's *theoria* or contemplation in Genesis after the conclusion of creation: "God saw everything that he had made, and indeed, it was very good" (Gen 1:31).[38] God rejoiced when he made humanity in his image.[39] Humanity could not and still cannot genuinely rejoice. We try to rejoice and ultimately end up like the actor Marlon Brando was said to utter on his deathbed about his life: "What the hell was that about?"

The Sabbath becomes the movement of God's enjoyment over what he has done. Since it is God's joy, creation is that which belongs to God, not just that which is given a purpose from God. The Sabbath is the testimony that we belong to God and therefore are invited to rest with God, to participate in his joy over creation, not to be anxious about fulfilling our "purpose." We rest because of God's vicarious rest, since we have not done any work from which to rest. This is grace at the heart of our creation, the world created through the Word of God, the second person of the Trinity, the eternal Son. The vicarious humanity of Christ (the vicarious rest of Christ?) is a reality even with God's rest as his response of joy over our creation.[40] We have a goal, Barth argues, but it is not that which can be attained by "toil and conflict but which is really granted" to us, a gift of grace. We are not just given a purpose, such as to have "dominion," to exercise dominion in light of what we have been given. The Son receives eternally from the Father in the Spirit that which is given to us. It is not up to us to fulfill our "purpose," even with God's help. God maintains his freedom in his initiative of rest as well as of creating.[41]

The very act of creating "lights," "evening," "morning," the "days" of creation are acts of differentiation for the sake of creating a space to relate to God, but not to be identified with him.[42] So also in the Trinity, God is not just a monad but truly in a perichoretic relationship, a relationship of mutual indwelling, "being in communion." Knowing the eternal Son in his

---

38. Macmurray, *The Self as Agent*, 194.
39. Barth, *CD* III/1: 99.
40. Ibid., 217–18.
41. Ibid., 226.
42. Ibid., 160–63, 170.

relationship to the Father through the Spirit enables us to look on creation in a new way. We can see creation now, in an aesthetic sense, through the eyes of the Son as he looks upon the Father, a relationship that is not just analogous to creation, but vicarious: he takes our place in dealing with God. Humanity is summoned to respond in decision, just as the Son is summoned to respond in decision by the Father. It is humanity, not fishes and birds, who can respond as this witness to God.[43] And in doing so, we see creation in all its beauty as formed by God's covenant and therefore a judgment on our purely utilitarian views of creation.

As Simon Chan argues, a "purpose-driven" theology reflects a view of the church that is only instrumentalist: the church is defined by what it does, the so-called "missional church," rather than by what it is, the body of Christ, incorporated into Christ, living an ontological connection to the Triune God.[44] Chan suggests that Niebuhr's "Christ and culture" models inevitably suppose that culture will determine the church, regardless if one chooses "Christ transforms culture" or "Christ against culture." The church is missional, but missional in an ontological way in its being as related to the continuing life and ministry of Jesus Christ. Remembering that Christ is the *leitourgos,* the minister in the sanctuary (Heb 8:2), worship (liturgy) should never be divorced from service (ministry). Any overemphasis on liturgy, as Chan seems to express, can reflect the lack of attention to the continuing humanity of Jesus Christ in ministry as our Priest and Minister, rather than worship and ministry being that which we do simply in memory of or in obedience to Jesus. Chan is also less helpful when he argues that the church should see itself as the fulfillment of creation. This seems to fall again into a kind of teleology in which the church simply fulfills the purpose of creation, rather than seeing the Triune God and his dynamic belonging between the Father and the Son in the Spirit as prior to creation, as the New Testament robustly sings, particularly in a Christological melody (John 1:3; Col 1:15–16; Heb 11:2). "The Lamb" was "slain from the foundation of the world," the old translation of Rev 13:8 goes (KJV), a favorite of supralapsarians. Supralapsarianism does not necessarily have to be deterministic, but can express that Irenaean theme that creation is first known in redemption. Contra Chan, Christ, not creation, is the backdrop for redemption. Creation is essentially not for any purpose, then, but done out of grace, an aesthetic movement of God.

43. Ibid., 175.
44. Chan, "Stopping the Cultural Drift," 67–69.

So attempts to discern a "purpose" for creation, even for human life, may be misdirected. Teleology has a long history in Christian thought (from Thomas Aquinas to the recent discussion over "intelligent design"), yet the joy of creation for God reminds us that God is not obsessed over "the purpose driven life," but enjoys the simple beauty of creation. Here we see the beautiful symphony of creation and grace, and the terrible problem when grace is restricted to redemption and salvation. The implications are also profound in a culture that values utility over everything else. "What use is that degree in English?" endures the harried liberal arts major. We may very well be restricting our humanity to intellectualism at the expense of our emotions if that is the case, Macmurray contends.

Can we read off God from creation? In its crudest form that is the perennial question of natural theology. The savoring of all beauty is a savoring of God, Hart argues (including a beautiful woman, according to Nicholas of Cusa).[45] The agony one feels is meant to turn us toward God, a thought not foreign to Augustine as well (*De musica* 6.10.29). Whereas Hart will admit that "None of this is to say that the soul can gain access to an immediate intuition of the divine form in the fabric of creation, unclouded by sin," he does allow for "a theological embrace of creation as a divine word precisely in its aesthetic excessiveness, its unforced beauty."[46] If by "theological" he means "by faith" (as in Heb 11:2: "By faith we understand that the worlds were prepared by the word of God . . . "), then we can agree. But his emphasis is elsewhere, on the somewhat grotesque imagery of "aesthetic excessiveness" (!). In contrast to this is the Lord's calm and steady response to his creation: "God saw everything that he had made, and indeed, it was very good" (Gen 1:31). But notice it is God's place to see and reflect, not ours. He responds vicariously, for us, to his own act of creation. This word is proclaimed to us by Jesus. In this, we have a gentle yet profound doctrine of creation. Christ's vicarious theology of creation has no need to be crushed by an "aesthetic excessiveness" that can only hide the personal act of God in Jesus Christ as we are buried under its heap. For Hart, creation itself is an expression of the joy of the Trinity, because "joy and love are its only grammar and its only ground."[47] But does God have any joy *at*, in response to creation, or is that left to us in a Pelagian fashion? Not so for the vicarious joy of Jesus, who rejoices with us and for us in a deep and rich appreciation

---

45. Hart, *The Beauty of the Infinite*, 254.
46. Ibid.
47. Ibid., 255.

for creation that we can only begin to approximate. His Eucharist is the true thanksgiving. Can creation tell us of God then? Of course. The eyes of Jesus see creation in a way that we can only hope to, but can never reach. We need his eyes, his aesthetics, his vision of God, and therefore of creation. Creation is ultimately mute without him. Hart wants to speak of creation as "a new emphasis" for God, and, in fact, God has always been Father, but he has not always been Creator.[48] Yet, according to Nicene faith, we are to know God as Creator through first knowing God as Father, "maker of heaven and earth." And this Father is only known through the faith and obedience of the Son who was made human, "for us and our salvation" (Nicaea), that is, vicariously, in our place and on our behalf.

Jesus brings us back to the joy that created us in the first place through his joy on our behalf. Most of the time real human beings do not live in a perfectly ordered universe suggesting "intelligent design," as much as we may desire that. No, in our honest moments we are constantly seeking to reconcile *hominum confusione et Dei providentia*, the confusion of humanity and the providence of God. Honesty with the confusion should not mean its mastery, however. These are not to be viewed as two equal elements, as Barth reminds us.[49] But why not? Why not simply become a Manichee, as a former colleague, once an evangelical pastor, blithely confessed to me: There are two eternal principles of good and evil; don't fight it, just live with it? The problem is that there is no one to speak for creation, for itself, apart from its utility.

Barth is careful, however, to remind us that there is an equal danger, promoted by the *hominem confusione*, in embracing "knowledge for the sake of knowledge, of power for the sake of power, of possession for the sake of possession, of glory for the sake of glory, of enjoyment for the sake of enjoyment."[50] The grim result of this is war. This is what happens with the continual autonomy of humanity, even a humanity that thinks it can balance the confusion of humanity and the providence of God (perhaps the most dangerous kind). *Creatio ex nihilo* reminds us that there is no existence without God, and therefore the creature is foolish to think that it has ultimate power over its existence, that we are in control, even that we

---

48. T. F. Torrance, *The Trinitarian Faith*, 90.
49. Barth, *CD* IV/3.2: 697–99.
50. Ibid., 699.

belong only to ourselves.[51] "We no longer think of ourselves as belonging to anyone or anything. We do not belong—we own; we possess."[52]

This is a sobering thought. In contrast to the belonging that exists between the Father and the Son for all eternity is our alienation, an anxious striving to possess: "The one who has the most toys in the end wins" reads the bumper sticker. I am not against possession, or even collecting (my collection of "Golden Age" and "Silver Age" comic books bears witness to that). But certainly our hobbies and our possessions often reflect the pathos and emptiness, and especially the lack of connectedness and belonging in our lives. Despair comes through a lack, even a perceived lack. But there is no lack in the relationship between the Father and the Son in which the Father loves the Son and the Son loves the Father (John 3:35; 5:19–20; 10:17; 15:9–10; 17:1, 4, 23, 26). The "inner life" of God is the basis of creation, the covenant, the pledge between the Father and the Son in the Spirit. Despair is created in us because we feel entitled to possess. Many have commented that the baby boomers are the generation of entitlement: we deserve all that we want. But the result of that craving for possession is amnesia, according to Elshtain: "Who are we? We are creatures who have forgotten what it means to be faithful to something other than ourselves."[53] The contrast cannot be greater if we consider Christ, "did not regard equality with God as something to be exploited, but emptied himself . . . " (Phil 2:6–7). Here again is our need for the vicarious obedience of Christ, without which we so easily fall into despair and stay there. We have pulled apart the twin movements of Augustine, as Jean Bethke Elshtain argues: *Frui*, "to enjoy and cling with love to something for its own sake" has become divorced from *uti*, "a form of use, employing something in order to obtain that which we love, providing it is worthy of love."[54] Is the combining of the two what is remarkable in the life and mission of Jesus? He "endured the cross," not for its own sake, but for the "joy set before him" (Heb 12:2). The cross was not simply endured because of his duty to the Father. Pain does not have a virtue in itself. He looked forward to the "joy." Yet joy was not a goal separated from his love and compassion for his lost sheep (Mark 6:34). Jesus brings the *frui* and the *uti* of creation together because we are unable to do so, and he does so through his vicarious joy in the midst of despair.

51. Barth, *CD* III/1: 7.
52. Elshtain, *Who Are We?*, 4.
53. Ibid.
54. Ibid., 53.

Theological Anthropology, Creation, and the Vicarious Joy of Christ

We may think that the aesthetic and religious possibilities speak loudest of what is truly wonderful about humanity. Barth surprisingly responds, "No!"[55] Barth does not see any virtue in simply exalting that which is empirically distinctive in the human person. For those distinctives can very easily leave out God. Who needs God when you have art and religion? And the history of humanity has born that out. What is left is the vicarious nature of God, so to speak. God does something we are unable to do for ourselves: He creates us. The vicarious humanity of Christ then is not far behind. For Christ reveals in his perfect faith and obedience to the Father in the Spirit that at the heart of what is truly human is our response-ability toward God.[56] The Son is the one addressed by the word of God. He is therefore truly human. Not far behind, of course, is true humanity as "co-humanity," not existing without the other. This response-ability is undertaken in society and on behalf of others (a "vicarious representative action," translating Bonhoeffer's word, *Stellvertretung*).[57] The "spirit," therefore, that Jesus commended to the Father on the cross is not a third part of his anthropology, but the "life-giving spirit" of "the last Adam" that Paul speaks of, a vicarious self, doing for others what they are unable to do for themselves (1 Cor 15:45).[58] We can live a quixotic existence of constantly searching for our "purpose" within ourselves rather than to accept our existence as God's gift, as objects of grace.[59]

We cannot control our own freedom and cannot bear our self-consciousness.[60] If there is one comment to make on the history of humanity it is that our freedom is out of control. It may express itself in the attempts by the few to absolutely control others or in a wild anarchy of the mob, but either way, we do not know what to do with our freedom. That is why it has become bondage, the *servum arbitrium* of Augustine, Luther, and Calvin. Our self-consciousness is the other prize possession of our modern selves. We are aware, and very proud of it. Both of these, however, are not pos-

---

55. Barth, *CD* III/2: 249 and Anderson, *On Being Human*, 33.
56. Anderson, *On Being Human*, 37.
57. Bonhoeffer, *Ethics*, 257–60, and *Sanctorum Communio*, 120, 146, 155, 182, 187.
58. Anderson, *On Being Human*, 38.
59. Barth, *CD* III/1: 95.
60. See Anderson, *On Being Human*, 39–40.

sessions, as we discover from the freedom and self-consciousness of Jesus Christ. He obtains these from the Father, and so our freedom and self-consciousness is therefore radically qualified by the Word of God that qualifies Jesus. The dilemma of freedom and determinism is broken by the power of God, as Anderson puts it, not by the resolution of logical gymnastics (rationalism) or ideological purity (Calvinism or Arminianism). Jesus himself is a person of "spiritual determinism": "This 'spiritual determinism' enables the human creature to do what no other creature can do—freely respond to another being out of one's own self."[61] What else could we conclude from the narratives of the Gospels? His human response comes "out of nothing," *ex nihilo*, not as his own possession or his own will (Gethsemane). To be human, therefore, is to live *ex nihilo*. Out of that *ex nihilo* comes this freedom to respond to another: God, the world, and others. Jesus' response to the Father is the foundation for our responses to God, the world, and the other person who is before us on the road. This is an *ex nihilo* experience which we should not come to with our own expectations, prejudices, biases, and preconceptions (the problem of the Pharisees and the Sadducees and the church throughout the ages). Otherwise, the possibility for relationship is doomed. Jesus Christ in his vicarious humanity is the essence of the reciprocal act that comes out of nowhere, out of nothing.[62] Out of this comes the fundamental structure of being human: "existence with regard to the other."[63] (Even the Lone Ranger had Tonto!) This is not to deny nor destroy individuality, but to establish it.[64] This radical proposal of Anderson's deserves much critical attention. But for now we need to observe that the vicarious humanity of Christ offers strong support for "the certain radical superiority . . . given to the 'we.'"[65] Whether or not Anderson will be able to sustain the individual is another matter, but that is at least his intention. The "I" is maintained because there is another. Christologically, that is found in the Son's response to the Father from all eternity, made manifest in the incarnation. "The 'I' is immanent in the 'Thou.'"[66] Or as Buber famously puts it, "I require a You to become; becoming I, I say you."[67]

61. Ibid., 40.
62. Ibid., 46.
63. Ibid., 44.
64. Ibid., 45.
65. Ibid.
66. Ibid., 46.
67. Buber, *I and Thou*, 62.

GOD'S JOY IN ACTION

Anderson contends that grace was from the beginning constituted as co-humanity.[68] In co-humanity, as seen paradigmatically in the humanity of Jesus, freedom as autonomy is not as important as what Anderson calls "discrimination."[69] Freedom can be easily misused by reaching out and touching someone indiscriminately. Pedophiles, sadists, and predators are only the grossest examples of that tendency in all of us. Discrimination, however, is not something we are born with; it has to come out of nothing, *ex nihilo*. Is that not true of all worthy virtues, as the "virtue theory" of ethics teaches us; habits that that must be created and trained in order to develop character? (Is this ethics *ex nihilo*?) Love can be misunderstood as simply "aesthetic excessiveness": "Love dies, not through lack of actions, but through lack of discrimination."[70] Our feeble attempts to create and maintain love ("All You Need is Love") are in stark contrast with the richness and self-giving of the eternal love of the Triune God revealed in the One who "emptied" himself (Phil 2:5). How much do we really want to *sacrifice* for the sake of the other? Is that lack the saddest manifestation of contemporary sexual obsessions?

We are not able to control the freedom of Jesus, "a living human person," and therefore grace is able to restore and heal creation: "Jesus Christ is a living human person who comes and speaks and acts with the claim and authority of God, and in relation to whom there can be no question whether of controlling or using him . . . "[71] Thus the providence of God over his creation is restored through the free act of the man Jesus who comes with the authority of God against our attempts at autonomy. The *ex nihilo* of creation is still in effect through the continuing grace of God in the person of Jesus Christ. There is an aesthetic *ex nihilo* in the movement of God in the incarnation, but it is the movement of God's glory returning through the face of Jesus in the Spirit in the vicarious faith of Christ.[72]

---

68. Anderson, *On Being Human*, 47.
69. Ibid., 63–64.
70. Ibid., 64.
71. Barth, *CD* IV/3.2: 706–7.
72. Anderson, *On Being Human*, 69.

CHAPTER FIVE

He Has Seen the Stars ... For Us

*The Vicarious Humanity of Christ,
the Priest of Creation*

"THEY HAVE NOT SEEN the stars" speaks Ray Bradbury of the non-human creation in his poem of the same name.[1] Of all the creatures in the world, humanity is privileged to know what it is seeing, to give voice to mute creation. So also, patristic and Orthodox theologies speak frequently of humanity as the priest of creation. What if we consider Christ in his humanity as the priest of creation in terms of T. F. Torrance's doctrine of the vicarious humanity of Christ? For Torrance, it is not simply the death of Christ that is vicarious, on our behalf and in our place, but the entirety of his life is atoning, his vicarious humanity that intercedes for us. Intercession is needed because "we do not know how to pray as we ought" (Rom 8:26). Intercession is not just an act of divine *fiat* but that which God takes from the side of our human nature, knowing our inability, in Jesus' vicarious faith, obedience, service, and prayer. This is God living a life of *advocacy* for us.[2] Such advocacy is that which reflects the trinitarian relationship of the Son before the Father, as the Son takes upon our human nature as our worship and prayer before God in both substitutionary and representative ways, recognizing our total need. As Torrance remarks, "That identification is so profound that through the Spirit Christ's prayers and intercessions are made to echo in our own, and there is no disentangling of them from our

---

1. Bradbury, "They Have Not Seen the Stars" from *They Have Not Seen the Stars: The Collected Poems of Ray Bradbury*, 259–60.
2. T. F. Torrance, *Atonement*, 275.

weak and stammering and altogether unworthy acts of devotion."[3] Barth reminds us to keep our eyes on Christ who prayed for us on the cross, not on our abilities to pray.[4] It is also a life of an eternal *offering* before the face of the Father, of which the incarnate life and obedience unto death is a mirror.[5] Offering is a part of the continuous intercession. "The offering is itself a continuous intercession: the continuous intercession implies the offering is a present thing."[6] As such there is a fusion between his divine and human life, a *continuing* life of Jesus Christ that lives before us, and all of creation, always. The *advocacy* of Christ has *ontological* content in the vicarious life of Christ and our union with him.

Key to the continuing life of Christ in our midst are the pictures of Jesus praying in Gethsemane, the Last Supper, the High Priestly prayer of John 17, and, of course, the Lord's Prayer, in which we "overhear" Christ pray so that he, in turn, may place these prayers in our mouths, not just as representative, but as substitute for our desperate neediness in prayer: "Lord, teach us to pray" (Luke 11:1).[7]

Not least among these priestly ministerings of Christ is his *benediction*, his blessings, most of all, in the Holy Spirit, the blessing of the ascended Christ (Acts 1:5; 2:33), recalling Melchizedek's blessing of Abraham (Gen 14:19, 20) and the Aaronic blessing of God's people (Num 6:24–26). "He ascended in order to fill all things with his person and bestow gifts of the Spirit upon men."[8]

The Epistle to the Hebrews speaks of "Jesus, a forerunner on our behalf," who has entered the sanctuary of the temple, "having become a high priest" (6:20). This priesthood lasts forever, so "he is able for all time to save those who approach God through him, since he always lives to make intercession for them" (7:24–25). "Holy, blameless, undefiled, separated from sinners, and exalted above the heavens" (7:26), yet he was "like his brothers and sisters in every respect" (2:14), one who can sympathize with our weaknesses (4:15). This priest is the Son (7:27–28), whose "more excellent ministry" than Moses is "the mediator of a better covenant" (8:1–6). In the "high priestly" prayer of Jesus in John 17, Jesus prays, "I sanctify

---

3. Ibid.
4. Barth, *A Karl Barth Reader*, 104.
5. T. F. Torrance, *Atonement*, 115.
6. Ibid., 116.
7. Ibid., 117.
8. Ibid., 118.

myself, so that they also may be sanctified in truth" (John 17:19), the One for the Many. There is no other sanctification apart from the sanctification of the Son. So there is no other human response apart from the human response of the Son. Therefore, Torrance can say, "Jesus Christ *is* our human response to God. Thus we appear before God and are accepted by him as those who are inseparably united to Jesus Christ our great High Priest in his eternal presentation to the Father."[9] As the one genuine human response, he "thereby invalidates all other ways of response."[10] Hence, the command to participate in the response of Jesus, to follow him, is in union with him, "one derived from, grounded in, and shaped by the very humanity of the Word which originally gave him being as man and continues to sustain him in his human nature and spontaneity before God as well as in his engagement in the world of things and persons to which he belongs," that is, creation.[11] He is the priest of creation, including human beings.

"Like his brothers in every respect"! How far is this true? Is he really the priest that Karl Barth and T. F. Torrance speak of, that even assumed fallen human nature, who reconciled even the human mind, in contrast to much of "evangelical" and religious rationalism of all ages?[12] How far then did God identify with his creation, in all of its "groanings" (Rom 8:23)? For only in plunging into the depths of the alienation of creation itself will there be its salvation. God's grace in creation will be his willingness to "get dirty" with his creation run amuck.

The challenge of possible ecological disaster and the problem of human culpability is rarely related to Christology. Regardless of the debates about the extent of human responsibility, for example, of global warming, no one would deny the fact that human beings, including human sin, affect the wider world around us, socially, physically, and spiritually. Often we are left with a social ethic that either restricts creation to a question of origins (on the right) or that all problems in nature can be solved by human ingenuity (on the left). We will not give answers to those questions here. But perhaps we can give a "prolegomenon" to a theology of nature based on a christological view of creation. Can we speak of Christ, the vicarious priest of creation, who can lead us to a better way? From a Christian perspective,

---

9. T. F. Torrance, *The Mediation of Christ*, 80.
10. T. F. Torrance, "The Word of God and the Response of Man," 145.
11. Ibid., 146.
12. T. F. Torrance, "Epilogue: The Reconciliation of Mind," *Atonement*, 440–47.

does Jesus know something about creation that we do not? Is it significant, therefore, to speak of Christ as the vicarious priest of creation?

Three theses are presented here: Christ the vicarious priest of creation is 1) the one obedient hearing human of the word of God, with perfect trust, joy, and worship (Luke 10:21), 2) the intersection between creation and redemption, and 3) the affirmation of creation, yet maintaining its distinction from God.

Christ the Priest: The One Obedient Human, Hearing the Word of God

First, Christ the vicarious priest of creation is the one obedient hearing human being of the word of God, with perfect trust, joy, and worship towards the Father. Kevin Vanhoozer and Douglas John Hall characterize the essential nature of human beings as speech agents. Yet if Christ is the revelation, not just of God, but of what it truly means to be human, then the obedient Son to the Father in the Gospels is not just the Word of God but also the Hearing Man.[13]

The vicarious obedient Son is first of all portrayed in the baptism of Jesus. Taking our human nature from us, Jesus' baptism is a sign of viewing the doctrine of baptism as one baptism, not just baptism as our response.[14] There is one "baptism," Torrance contends, that includes "the whole historical Jesus Christ from his birth to his resurrection and ascension," all consisting his vicarious humanity, in which we participate.[15] So baptism should not be seen as either simply a ritual or ethical act, but a participation in Christ's baptism.[16] Torrance refers to this "dimension of depth" as an imperative to "look away from ourselves."[17] Yet this does not leave our individual reality behind, because "as Jesus Christ is, so we are in the world."[18] Since we are ontologically involved in his priesthood, we cannot avoid him. That is the glory, and responsibility, of baptism.

---

13. Vanhoozer, "Human Being, Individual and Social," 175, and Hall, *Imaging God*, 204–5.

14. See T. F. Torrance, "The One Baptism Common to Christ and His Church," *Theology in Reconciliation*, 82–105.

15. Ibid., 82.

16. Ibid., 83.

17. Ibid., 89.

18. Ibid.

The baptism of Jesus is one portrayal of the obedience of Jesus to the Father that is a reality for the entirety of his life "the whole course of his obedience" and "the whole life of Christ," as Calvin states, while reserving the "peculiar and proper" place to Christ's death.[19]

Prayer, obedient prayer, begins with the Lord's Prayer, the "Our Father," which is Jesus' prayer to the Father that he enables us to pray with him. For apart from him we cannot pray to the Father in obedience. There is a substitutionary element in prayer that is often neglected but can be seen in the vicarious humanity of Christ, in his vicarious life of obedience lived for us. Torrance portrays this vividly: "While sinners we are unable to pray to the Father as we ought, yet the Lord Jesus Christ in his self-submission and self-offering to the Father, has put his prayer, *Our Father*, into our unclean mouth, so that we may pray through him and with and in him to the Father . . . "[20]

As Ray Anderson suggests, the Word of God creating Adam is the sole source of Adam and Eve's "response-ability."[21] The speech of God creates the hearing human. Is the sinful human predicament not so much our lack of speaking but a lack of silence for the sake of hearing? Having heard perfectly the word of the Father, Christ the priest of creation is then able to articulate the cries of creation, just as the priest represents the people. His difference is in the vicarious element. Not only does he represent the people, but because of the sin of humanity, he takes their place as the perfect priest, for the sake of all creation, especially abused creation such as nature and animals (and abused women and children, one may add). Origen, taught by Paul that "all things, whether on earth or in heaven" had been reconciled by Christ (Col 1:20), declared that Christ is "the great High Priest not for the sake of humankind alone but for every being, offering himself as a sacrificial offering once and for all" (*In Ioannem* 1.40, PG 14.93).[22]

As priest, Christ in his unique humanity *(enhypostasia)*, rather than overriding our will, frees our humanity for genuine human decision and human response in relation to the truth of God's grace.[23] The crucial question, as a young T. F. Torrance observed, is whether we are going to see, in

---

19. Calvin, *Institutes*, 2.16.5. Cf. T. F. Torrance, *Scottish Theology*, 138–39; Heppe, *Reformed Dogmatics*, 458–59.

20. T. F. Torrance, *Scottish Theology*, 306.

21. Anderson, *On Being Human*, 82–83.

22. O'Collins and Jones, *Jesus Our Priest*, 72.

23. T. F. Torrance, *Theological Science*, 218.

our humanity through Christ's eyes, or not, "unless we exercise our will through the Will of Christ."[24]

What does it means for Christ to be the obedient human being who hears the word of God? On behalf of all of creation, including humanity, his objective confession of faith becomes the basis for our confession of sin. In Torrance's words, "Jesus' confession before Pilate and on the cross is the counterpart to his heavenly confession before the Father."[25] He is also the one who in solidarity with us vicariously confesses our sins in his baptism (Matt 3:13–17; Luke 3:21–22). This objective confession of Christ the priest is given its subjective counterpart in the subjective confession in the worship and confession of the church.[26] Yet this is never to be seen to be done without the living continuing life of Christ, the ascended One who, exalted by the Father, has poured forth his Spirit (Acts 2:33). Therefore, the "perfection" of creation is done by the continuing presence of Christ, not by a "perfection" of Christ. He and his work do not need to be perfected. But he does continue to unveil *(apocalypsis)* the healing that has already happened ontologically in Christ, as Jesus touched the lepers and they were made clean (Mark 1:42).

Christ is the priest who is truly human on behalf of creation and becomes a judge of our inappropriate domination of creation. Only God can create the capacity within us to hear and know him, a "human co-efficient" to make us partners with him.[27] This "two-way" relationship is inevitably an anthropomorphic model, yet does not have to be anthropocentric, Torrance argues, if God is on both sides of the relationship in the vicarious humanity of Christ. In Christ the priest God gives himself to us in our categories, in order for us to be lifted up in our humanity and adopted to him, renouncing ourselves, if we are truly to follow and love him.[28] These unavoidable anthropomorphisms do not absolve the human knower of the need to be self-critical and self-corrective of all "inappropriate anthropomorphisms."[29] In fact, one might even say that Christ the priest who proclaims the word as well as provides the perfect response in his true human obedience to the

---

24. T. F. Torrance, *The Doctrine of Jesus Christ*, 90; Cf. Molnar, *Thomas F. Torrance*, 116.

25. T. F. Torrance, *Atonement*, 90.

26. Ibid., 91.

27. T. F. Torrance, "The Christian Apprehension of God the Father," 124.

28. Ibid., 127.

29. Ibid., 128.

Father judges our false attempts at being priests of creation, often reflected as patronizing attempts to "save" nature. (Why do we think *we* know best?)[30]

The Epistle to the Hebrews speaks of Jesus as both "the apostle and high priest of our confession" (Heb 3:1), one who was "faithful to the one who appointed him as Moses was also faithful in all God's house" (Heb 3:2). "Confession" here obviously is connected with "faithfulness," tying together "apostle" and "high priest." Jesus' life is one sent from God (apostle) but also to respond to God on behalf of humanity, as their priest (high priest), a "double movement," the double movement of the incarnation, the second movement being that of the vicarious humanity of Christ.[31]

As our high priest, Christ's confession is that which enables us to "hold fast to our confession" (Heb 4:14), and to "approach the throne of grace with boldness" (Heb 4:16), that is, the *hilasterion*, the mercy seat of the holy of holies, with the sprinkled blood of the covenant of the priest who himself has now become the victim.[32] Christ's confession has become our confession, his answer to the Father has become our answer. "It is therefore the confession of our hopes, for all our hope rests upon the obedience of Christ and his vicarious confession before the face of the Father."[33] We give voice on behalf of all of creation to those hopes in our worship of thanksgiving and praise.

Central to the implications of the confession of Christ for creation is this: as Torrance puts it: "the very voice that condemns us is also the voice that freely forgives us."[34] The possible staggering cosmological implications of this should not be missed. Is there judgment on creation? Does the cosmos need to be forgiven? We do not know. Short of saying that God (or Satan) "caused" natural evil, what we do know is that what God creates is good (Gen 1). We must remain ignorant of the origin of creation's "groanings" (Rom 8:22). We only know that there is something wrong. Creation needs an Advocate. Yea, the *Cosmos*, especially thinking of ordered creation, needs an Advocate. But the one who condemns is also the one who forgives. There is no doubt here, no separation of justice and love. The cosmic harmony is in the heart of God. The confession is made in onto-

---

30. See Ferguson, *The Cosmos and the Creator*, 72.

31. T. F. Torrance, *Atonement*, 89. Cf. T. F. Torrance, *Conflict and Agreement in the Church, Volume II*, 69.

32. T. F. Torrance, *Atonement*, 91.

33. Ibid.

34. Ibid., 92.

logical, not just functional, connection to our humanity. As Ray Anderson expresses it, "this means that the relation of Jesus as obedient Son to God as loving and sending Father has its origin within the very being of God's existence."[35] The implications are profound if we take Christ's confession as the basis for our confession in order to approach the throne of grace with boldness (Heb 4:14–16): "Only if the incarnation provides an ontological and not merely functional relation to God through the life of this man will we have assurance of God's gracious provision for humans to share in God's own divine and eternal life."[36] To speak of Jesus as only a "parable" of God will not do! A priest has an ontological relation, at the level of being *(ontos)* with both his people and creation, not just a function.

Reconciliation with humanity and the cosmos comes even at the depths of God-forsakenness, as we know from the cry of abandonment from the cross: "My God, my God, why have you forsaken me" (Matt 27:46). Does this mean there was a split in the being of the Godhead? No, there is never a disharmony between the Father and the Son, for the Son goes willingly to the cross, led by the Spirit. But he does go to the depths of our forsakenness. He is the priest who becomes the sacrifice. That is the depth of his assumption of our humanity.[37] The "wonderful exchange" (Calvin, *Inst.* 4.17.2) that we even celebrate in the Lord's Supper, Calvin says, is done by God himself. That is the meaning of *reconciliation* in the Bible: *exchange,* a substitutionary, vicarious word, meaning an ontological reality. "Christ is so one with God that what he did God did, and so one with us that what he did we did."[38]

The obedience of Christ is not limited to the first century. His obedient, priestly life continues today, and neglecting that can lead to a mishandling often of the text of the New Testament, Torrance contends. In fact "the basic text" of revelation is not the New Testament but "the obedient humanity of Jesus Christ."[39] Apostolic tradition functions rightly when it recognizes the continuous life of Jesus Christ, his living priesthood, and the New Testament text as an indispensable yet relative "glass" or "window" into the living humanity of Christ. "The New Testament is the inspired

---

35. Anderson, "The Incarnation of God in Feminist Christology," 307.
36. Ibid., 308.
37. T. F. Torrance, *Atonement,* 150.
38. Ibid., 152.
39. Ibid., 340.

secondary text" is the way Torrance puts it.⁴⁰ The important point is that Christ the priest uses the New Testament text himself in an active way. He is not just the object of the text. He has a priestly ministry in reading Scripture, in effect.

As the Fathers, Eastern Orthodox theologians, and T. F. Torrance stress, humanity has that unique role as "priest of creation," able to articulate that which nature cannot express.⁴¹ We actually see the stars, as Ray Bradbury rhapsodizes. However, as with Spider-Man, with great power comes great responsibility! The descent and ascent in the incarnation (see Phil 2:5–11) is one that God makes. The human tendency is to bypass the hearing, speaking, and confessing of the Son and to present our ascent to God as the condition for God's descent, as in the spiritual tradition of ascending the mountain as found in Gregory of Nyssa.⁴² By contrast, T. F. Torrance strongly argues for the teaching of Athanasius: Christ "became Mediator between God and men in order that he might minister the things of God to us and the things of ours to God."⁴³ "The things of ours" are presented by Christ the priest, reflecting the precursor in the levitical priesthood, in which all Israel enters into the sanctuary in the person of the High Priest, confessing the sins of the people (see also the baptism of Jesus).⁴⁴ James Torrance, citing Calvin on Hebrews, "The ascended Lord leads our songs and is the chief composer of our hymns."⁴⁵ In addition, Jesus prays, on earth and in heaven (Heb 7:25: "he lives to make intercession").⁴⁶ As the Orthodox theologian Alexander Schmemann comments, "Only in Him can we say Amen to God, or rather He himself is our Amen to God . . ."⁴⁷ In the Scottish theologian John McLeod Campbell's words, Christ uttered "a perfect amen in humanity to the judgment of God on the sins of man."⁴⁸

---

40. Ibid.

41. Clément, *The Roots of Christian Mysticism*, 77.

42. Gregory of Nyssa, *The Life of Moses II*, 12–17. See the criticism in T. F. Torrance, *Royal Priesthood*, 39–40. Cf. Christ as confessor in Hebrews (3:1; 4:14; 10:23) in T. F. Torrance, *Royal Priesthood*, 12, 39–40, 46, 56.

43. *Contra Arianos*, 4:6., cited in T. F. Torrance, "The Paschal Mystery of Christ and the Eucharist," *Theology in Reconciliation*, 110, n. 1.

44. James B. Torrance, "The Priesthood of Jesus," 169–70.

45. On Calvin's interpretation of Heb 2:12 in James B. Torrance, "The Vicarious Humanity of Christ and the Priesthood of Christ in the Theology of John Calvin," 69–84.

46. Barth, *CD* II/2: 178. Cf. Origen, *On Prayer* 10–11.

47. Schmemann, *For the Life of the World*, 29.

48. Campbell, *The Nature of the Atonement*, 118.

Hearing, speaking, confessing, singing and praying all belong to Christ, on our behalf, and on behalf of creation. Christ reveals the fulfillment of the human being as created to be priest of creation, although we fail so badly at that task, often disabling nature's praise of God: the hills and the valleys shouting and singing together with joy (Ps 65:12–13). Through Christ, nature sings again.

The Fathers and Eastern Orthodox theology frequently speak of humanity as a "microcosm" of creation, the creation in miniature, with implications of human beings as mediators for the sake of creation.[49] So also T. F. Torrance speaks of the rational articulation that humanity as priest is meant to give for creation as a "mediator of order."[50] The seventh century theologian, Maximus the Confessor, prefers to speak of humanity as "macrocosmos," in order to stress the responsibility in comprehending the cosmos, a reflection of humanity being in the image of God.[51] Barth resists speaking of humanity as a microcosm of creation. For Barth, this is to confuse anthropology with cosmology and place the totality of creation's meaning with humanity.[52] One manifestation of the hubris of humanity is a self-image that ignores the wider cosmos. Nonetheless, Barth contends that the creation exists for humanity, "the sun by day and the moon by night shine for him."[53] The human is, in fact, as with Maximus' "macrocosm," "the object of God's purposes for the cosmos."[54] Nonetheless, whether as "microcosm," "macrocosm," or as "the object of God's purposes for the cosmos," how easily can the hubris of humanity develop an arrogance against the rest of creation.

Barth, however, can surprisingly speak of Christ as a "cosmic being," in the sense that his humanity exists for others, a vicarious humanity.[55] "In light of the man Jesus," Barth contends, "man is the cosmic being." Perhaps the distinctiveness and value of humanity can be affirmed in terms of Christ the vicarious priest. Christ's vicarious priesthood is a priesthood first of

---

49. Ware, *The Orthodox Way*, 53–55; George Kehm, "Priest of Creation," 129–30.

50. T. F. Torrance, "Man, Mediator of Order" in *The Christian Frame of Mind*, 35–64.

51. Louth, "The Cosmic Vision of Saint Maximus the Confessor," 186–87; Staniloae, *Orthodox Dogmatic Theology*, Vol. 1, 4; Clément, *The Roots of Christian Mysticism*, 77; Thunberg, *Man and the Cosmos*, 74; Maximus the Confessor, *Mystalogia*, 7, and "The Church's Mystalogy," 196–97.

52. Barth, *CD* III/2: 15–16.

53. Ibid., III/4: 573.

54. Ibid., II/2: 16.

55. Ibid., III/2: 208.

all for humanity, but for the purpose that humanity would not ignore the whole of God's creation. Indeed, the irony is that the hubris of humanity necessitates its priority in Christ's redemptive concerns, for the sake of the wider creation. The eucharistic joy of the only One who truly gives thanks to the Father ("Jesus rejoiced . . . and said, 'I thank you, Father . . . " Luke 10:21) is an invitation to participate in his thanksgiving for nature, animals and the glory of God's creation.[56]

The Orthodox theologian John Zizioulas, Metropolitan of Pergamon, argues for humanity as priest of creation yet criticizes what he perceives as Torrance's overly rationalistic definition, centered on scientific endeavor. The creative nature of human priesthood of creation is that which will save us from ecological woes, according to Zizioulas.[57] A scientific, and therefore technological, worldview is the source of much of our problems for Zizioulas. Torrance, however, possesses a much more subtle perspective than just a pragmatic or instrumentalist view of science. For him, genuine science does not involve an outdated Enlightenment view of mastery over nature, but a respectful atttitude, allowing that which you seek to know to disclose itself to you, whether that be nature, human beings, or God.[58] In Torrance's words, "Man acts rationally only under the compulsion of reality and its intrinsic order, but it is man's specific vocation to bring it to words, to articulate it in all its wonder and beauty, and thus to lead the creation to its praise and glorification of God the Creator."[59]

Christ "recapitulates," "sums up" the entirety of humanity, in Irenaeus' theology - a priestly act - including the intellective as well as the creative aspect through the scientific and medical endeavor of restoring order and creating reconciliation.[60] David Bentley Hart is right that "Christ must retell" the true story of the world, but wrong in his belief that Christ's recapitulation is predicated upon an analogy of being between God and humanity.[61] Christ the priest interrupts any such search or need for an analogy

---

56. See Barth *CD* III/2: 214. Cf. Ware, *The Orthodox Way*, 54.

57. Zizioulas, "Preserving God's Creation," 5. Cf. Gunton, *Christ and Creation*, 120–21.

58. T. F. Torrance, *The Ground and Grammar of Theology*.

59. T. F. Torrance, *Reality and Evangelical Theology*, 26–27. Cf. "The Goodness and Dignity of Man in the Christian Tradition," 322.

60. T. F. Torrance, *Divine and Contingent Order*, 130–31.

61. David Bentley Hart, *The Beauty of the Infinite*, 269: "In God desire both evokes and is evoked; it is one act that for us can be grasped only by analogy to the constant dynamism within our being that comprises the distinct but inseparable moments of interior and exterior splendor." Cf. 325.

that does not insist on the total need of humanity in its hubris for a priest who is not only a representative but also a substitute. Christ's "retelling" is substitutionary, but not to be restricted exclusively to a penalty for sin.[62] The Epistle to the Hebrews reminds us of the uniqueness of Christ's priesthood: He is the priest who is also the sacrifice; not just representing the people, but becoming their substitute in every way. Otherwise, his offering is only another form of religion, our attempts to be our own priests.[63]

Harold H. Oliver and H. Paul Santmire criticize twentieth century Protestant thought for ignoring a theology of creation for the sake of redemption.[64] Indeed, a theology that speaks of God and human relations alone is judged by Christ the priest of creation.[65] In Schmemann's words, Christ reveals the essence of priesthood as love, not religious control.[66] The articulation of creation by Christ allows creation to become itself, not to be exploited, much less to be destroyed. Scientific duty can then become a deeply religious duty before God.[67]

Christ the Priest: The Intersection of Creation and Redemption

Secondly, Christ the vicarious priest of creation is the intersection between creation and redemption. The doctrine of creation out of nothing is upheld by the Priest who is also the Word of God by whom all things came into being (John 1:3). William Dyrness is right to argue for the integration of creation and redemption.[68] Yet is he tempted to hold to a priority of creation before redemption, of nature before grace? Kathryn Tanner repeats the characteristic objection to Barth's Christocentrism. For Barth, according

---

62. T. F. Torrance, *Space, Time, and Resurrection*, 116; *Theology in Reconciliation*, 133–34.

63. Redding, *Prayer and the Priesthood of Christ in the Reformed Tradition*, 298 n. 31; T. F. Torrance, *Theology in Reconstruction*, 167–68.

64. Oliver, "The Neglect and Recovery of Nature in Twentieth Century Protestant Thought," 379, 381; Santmire, *The Travail of Nature*.

65. T. F. Torrance, *Reality and Evangelical Theology*, 25–26.

66. Schmemann, *For the Life of the World*, 93.

67. Cf. T. F. Torrance, *Reality and Evangelical Theology*, 26–27: "Man acts rationally only under the compulsion of reality and its intrinsic order, but it is man's specific vocation to bring it to words, to articulate it in all its wonder and beauty, and thus to lead the creation in its praise and glorification of God the Creator."

68. Dyrness, *The Earth is God's*, 27.

to Tanner, "Revelation in Christ seems to be not just one place where the gracious prevenient initiative of God is manifest, but the only place."[69] A consequent devaluation of ordinary experience is the result, in which God is absent. The vicarious humanity of Christ is dominant in many ways throughout Barth's theology, but an emphasis on the exalted and ascended humanity of Christ the priest, neglected in Barth, as T. F. Torrance points out, could provide a response to such objections.[70] Christ the priest argues against a "naked" theology of creation that does not presuppose grace. In Christ, grace is not the perfection of nature, as in both medieval theology and Federal Calvinism, but its fulfillment. The promise of humanity as microcosm/macrocosm has been fulfilled, not just perfected. Otherwise, nature becomes the standard that defines grace.[71] Christ the priest reveals that grace is the word even before the event of the cosmos. Creation and redemption are wedded together because of the priority of grace seen in the vicarious humanity of Christ.

Justification by faith, therefore, is not disconnected from the doctrine of creation. The priestly work of Christ tells of an eloquence about the cosmos that needs to be heard because Christ has seen something we have failed to see. The same is true of human inability to save ourselves, to give meaning to life and rescue from death. The *ex nihilo* of creation is, as Colin Gunton suggests, language that speaks of God acting without any source from outside of himself, a radically different kind of cosmology.[72] Creation out of nothing means that creation is utterly dependent upon God. The same is true for salvation. Faith, according to Hilary of Poitiers, is an acknowledgment of our incompetence to apprehend the inexhaustible God.[73] Sarah's barrenness in the Genesis story becomes the occasion for faith.[74]

Christ the priest offers and proclaims the *ex nihilo* by which both creation and redemption occur. His priestly action, therefore, includes not leaving nature to its fate nor assuming that human ingenuity can create

---

69. Tanner, "Jesus Christ," 266.

70. See T. F. Torrance on Barth and ascended humanity of Christ: "My Interaction with Karl Barth," 62; *Karl Barth: Biblical and Evangelical Theologian*, 134.

71. James B. Torrance, "Introduction" to John McLeod Campbell, *The Nature of the Atonement*, 6.

72. Gunton, "The Doctrine of Creation," 141–42.

73. Hilary of Poitiers, *On the Trinity*, 2.11.

74. Anderson, *The Soul of Ministry*, 43–51.

a utopia. The genuine scientist, T. F. Torrance reminds us, seeks to know things according to their natures ("nature is to be respected and courted, not imposed upon"),[75] and therefore, is dedicated to a moral agenda: working towards how things ought to be.[76] In Pauline language, creation is "groaning," longing to be "set free from its bondage to decay" (Rom 8:21). Christ the priest is working on behalf of his creation through obtaining "the freedom of the glory of the children of God" (Rom 8:21). According to Torrance, reconciliation, the unifying of soul and body, the sensible and the intelligible, happens in the articulate obeying of the Son, the Priest.[77] This offering of his humanity to the Father is continuous, although the shedding of his blood is a one time event.[78] Thus, Zizioulas must be questioned when he refers to Christ's priestly role as having now been "assigned to the Church," though the church offers "through the priestly action of Christ."[79] Even though the church is his body, the church is not the head. As Gunton points out, Zizioulas' emphasis on humanity as priest in terms of creative ability may overstress human activity.[80] The vicarious priesthood of Christ warns against this and stresses first of all the relatedness between the Father and the Son, not creativity, as the essence of the priesthood of humanity.[81]

Christ the Priest: The Affirmation of, Yet Distinction from Creation

Thirdly, Christ the vicarious priest of creation is the affirmation of creation, yet maintaining its distinction from God. What difference does the vicarious priesthood of Christ make for creation? Is a harmony or reconciliation of creation predicated upon a kind of panentheism in which the world is God's "body," a part of God (process theology)? Does maintaining

---

75. T. F. Torrance, *The Ground and Grammar of Theology*, 10. Cf. Jeremy Begbie in regards to creativity and art: not a movement from the artist to the world, but "a sense of the priority of reception over imposition," based on the vicarious humanity of Christ." *Voicing Creation's Praise*, 257.

76. T. F. Torrance, *The Christian Frame of Mind*, 53.

77. T. F. Torrance, *Transformation and Convergence in the Frame of Knowledge*, 337. Cf. "The Goodness and Dignity of Man in the Christian Tradition," 322.

78. Redding, *Prayer and the Priesthood of Christ in the Reformed Tradition*, 72.

79. Zizioulas, Metropolitan John of Pergamon, "Man the Priest of Creation," 184–85.

80. Gunton, *Christ and Creation*, 120.

81. Ibid., 121.

a distinction between God and creation (Reformed theology) inevitably communicate an aloof, transcendent God and a creation that can be exploited and abused?

Religious fatalism and secular utopian confidence both fail to do justice to Jesus Christ in his continuing ministry as priest of creation, fulfilling the human destiny as made in the image of God to enable creation to know itself. Only human beings can see the stars, know what they see.[82] This is not a "rationalistic" mastery over nature, as Zizioulas criticizes Torrance, using creation for an alien end, a "tormenting of nature," which Torrance rejects, but to give articulation to nature, "pregnant with new forms of being." Christ the priest is the Son of the Father, so he is doing this in harmony, in relationship with the Father, not in a brash activity of capricious creativity. Nor is he compelled by his interactions with creation in a panentheistic sense. The Son acts in freedom because he is *homoousios* with the Father, of the same substance, participating in the only genuine freedom of the personhood of God.[83] Creation can become free and humanity can become free because God is free, as Barth comments.[84] Christ the priest continues to freely offer the creation to the Father in the Spirit and is always a judgment on our attempts at priesthood apart from him.

Christ's continual ministry as priest, the ascended Lord through whom the Father sends the Spirit, does so in terms of a community, his body, the church. The tendency at times to restrict his priesthood to only a celestial omnipotence ignores the presence of Christ the vicarious priest in his continual offering in the Eucharist, the offering of thanksgiving, as first of all, his offering, not ours, one we are invited to join together in with him.[85] "The ministry of the community," Barth contends, "is Christ's ministry of both speech and action."[86] "The Christian community exists as He, Jesus Christ, exists. It does not exist merely because He exists."[87] The disciples were not meant to pass on their own witness but the "self-witness" of Christ. This involves the action of the priest as not only offering, but

---

82. T. F. Torrance, *Reality and Evangelical Theology*, 26.

83. Alan Torrance, *Persons in Communion*, 35.

84. Barth, *CD* III/1: 13–15.

85. Jungmann, "The High Priest and the Eucharist," *The Place of Christ in Liturgical Prayer*, 254, 257. Cf. Redding, *Prayer and the Priesthood of Christ in the Reformed Tradition*, 72.

86. Barth, *CD* IV/3.2: 862. Barth cites Matt 9:35; Luke 4:43, 24:19; Acts 10:28.

87. Ibid., 754.

also speech. In the levitical priesthood, the priest was the teacher of the law, so the priesthood of Christ does not exclude this voice, articulating for humanity and creation what they are unable to say as well as do.[88] This articulation includes the priestly blessing of Num 6:24: "The Lord bless you and keep you . . ."[89] The point here is that this is a living ministry, through the church, but not "assigned" to the church. In the vicarious humanity of Christ, Jesus fulfills as well as gives the promise, a challenge to both the neglect of nature and secular self-salvation.[90]

Christ the vicarious priest continues his "remedial and integrative activity," in T. F. Torrance's words.[91] This includes the whole of creation, but beginning with the whole human being. Athanasius sees this as the significance of the incarnation: "The Saviour having in very truth become man, the salvation of the whole man was brought about . . . Truly our salvation is no myth, and does not extend to the body only—the whole man, body and soul, has truly received salvation in the Word himself."[92] The vicarious priesthood of Christ, both as representative and substitute, reaffirms this expanse of healing and salvation, even beyond humanity to all of creation, as in Paul, for whom God through Christ "was pleased to reconcile to himself all things, whether on earth or in heaven" (Col 1:20).

The "groanings," the despair of the cosmos, are brought to the Father by the One who cried from the cross, "My God, my God why have you forsaken me?" Creation is not to feel guilty because it cries out, for its High Priest cries out as well. Alan Lewis reminds us that a theology of Holy Saturday means that the church, as the body of Christ, participates in his buried, Holy Saturday body.[93] The suffering church is the "holy priesthood" of I Peter 2:5, made "a kingdom, priests serving [their] God and Father" (Rev 1:6; cf. 5:10; 20:6), not any cause for triumphalism. These priests only share in Christ's priesthood.[94] But they do share. They are not inactive. They are active as he continues to be active. Yet they are not to be nervous in their activity, for they first participate in the prayers of Christ the High Priest, prayers in the midst of mission, not as incidental to mission.

88. James B. Torrance, "The Priesthood of Jesus," 169.
89. Ware, *The Orthodox Way*, 53–54.
90. Barth, *CD* IV/4: 196, on baptism.
91. T. F. Torrance, *Divine and Contingent Order*, 130; cf. *Royal Priesthood*, 37.
92. Athanasius, *Ad Epict.*, 7; cited by T. F. Torrance, *The Trinitarian Faith*, 152.
93. Alan E. Lewis, *Between Cross and Resurrection*, 388, 398.
94. *Lumen Gentium*, 10 from *Vatican Council II*, 361.

The mission of the "holy priesthood," therefore, is not to be separated from its nature as community, certainly as a reflection of the triune God, but also as a reflection of the vicarious priest. As John Macmurray reminds us, the infant is absolutely dependent on the community as one comes into the world.[95] Human existence at its core can be seen as *vicarious existence*. Christ the priest is creating communities that reflect dependence on God as the creative possibility of genuine, not neurotic (panentheistic?), dependence on one another.[96] Therefore the necessity of the church as a liturgical community is deeper and broader than we might think, as Ray Anderson suggests. This may include hospitality, acts of forgiveness, Sabbath rest and other rituals that reinforce personhood.[97] Priestly intercession may even involve interceding for those abused in our society (the intercessor as advocate).[98] This should be the "holy priesthood's" existence until the Lamb takes the place of the light of the city of God, of even the created lights, so that Christ the priest, in Barth's words, "will be His own witness" (Rev 21:23f.; 22:50).[99]

---

95. Macmurray, *Persons in Relation*, 49–50.
96. Cf. Barth, *CD* I/2: 385, 421, 431.
97. Anderson, *On Being Human*, 181.
98. Anderson, *Self-Care*, 137–38.
99. Barth, *CD* III/1: 121. Previous versions of this essay were given at the March 5, 2006 Southwest meeting of the American Academy of Religion in Dallas, Texas and in the Vol. 5, 2015 issue of *Participatio*, the on-line journal of the Thomas F. Torrance Theological Fellowship (www.tftorrance.org). My thanks to the editor of *Participatio*, Todd Speidell, and the referee of the article, for their constructive suggestions.

CHAPTER SIX

"For I Do Not Do the Good I Want... And I'm Tired of Trying"

Weakness and the Vicarious Humanity of Christ

ONE OF RAY ANDERSON'S most creative contributions to theology has been in theological anthropology. I can well remember the spiritual and theological excitement I felt when I first read *On Being Human: Essays in Theological Anthropology* (1982)![1] From the issues of abortion to homosexuality, Anderson was right to see that the study of theological anthropology would be a remedy for the continual confusion the church faces in these areas.

A later of book of Anderson's, however, building upon and elaborating on his theological anthropology, has not received all the attention it deserves. *Self-Care: A Theology of Personal Empowerment and Spiritual Healing* (1995) develops the profound implications of a theological anthropology in terms of both a theology of emotions, often sadly neglected in traditional theology, and in addressing existential crises such as shame and abuse.[2] My own work in recent years in drawing out the implications of the vicarious humanity of Christ for existential crises has found rich resources in Anderson's pioneering work. Among these issues is the problem of weakness. Early in Ray's theological career, the British theologian D.M. Mackinnon paid tribute to the "nervous, restless quality" of Anderson's writing and the "breadth and depth of his theological culture" which "entices the reader

---

1. Anderson, *On Being Human*.
2. Anderson, *Self-Care*.

83

to engage himself or herself with the issues with which he is concerned."[3] This essay is one modest attempt also to pay tribute to a career of "nervous, restless" theology, from which this writer has greatly benefited![4]

The Problem and Denial of Weakness

Self-esteem is a popular topic. Why shouldn't it be? Who can deny our need for self-esteem? Few among us have not been battered down by the criticisms and demands of others and ourselves. If we could just affirm our self-worth, perhaps we can live healthy lives, not haunted by the grim spectres of our failures and our inability to live up to expectations often impossible for us to fulfill.

But why am I so susceptible to the accusing finger that tells me that I have failed? Perhaps it is because I am too aware of my weakness. I see myself in Bernanos' country priest, the very picture of ineptitude. I see myself even at times as Green's "whiskey priest" in *The Power and the Glory*, living a life of hypocrisy. I see myself as Kafka's "K.," a helpless victim of the external forces of life and fate, which I can neither understand nor control. I see myself as King Lear, a prideful, self-centered king who tries to evade responsibility but wants the power and the authority and the acclaim at the same time. Scripture testifies itself that "while we were still weak, at the right time Christ died for the ungodly" (Rom 5:6). The disciples only represent all of us when they fail to heed Jesus' instructions to "stay awake" in Gethsemane (Matt 26:41). They do not stay awake, and only prove Jesus' following comment, "The spirit indeed is willing but the flesh is weak." But this can only reaffirm to me what a miserable creature I am. The result is that I almost drown in my weakness. I become a weak, pitiful figure.

How can I still say that I am a Christian? How can I live with myself in all this weakness? How can I expect others to like, let alone love me, in my weakness? And how can God put up with such a pitiful ambassador?

My weakness may take many forms. Paul's admonition to the Thessalonians to "help the weak" is probably engendered by their weariness in waiting for the Second Coming (1 Thess 5:14; 4:13–18).[5] The physical exis-

---

3. D. M. Mackinnon, foreword to Anderson, *Historical Transcendence and the Reality of God*, ix.

4. I would like to thank Todd Speidell for careful criticism of an earlier version of this essay.

5. Black, *Paul, Apostle of Weakness*, 46.

tence itself is an obvious source of basic human weakness. Paul makes the point to the Corinthians that, even though there will be a resurrected body, first the body "is sown in weakness" and "dishonor" (1 Cor. 15:43). Paul's "weakness of the flesh" (literally, Gal. 4:13) is probably not his emotional frailties but a "physical infirmity" (so NRSV).[6]

Such frailty is not simply physical. The physical and the emotional join hand in hand. The felt omnipotence of the newborn infant and its need for self-fulfillment is soon frustrated, as Ray Anderson points out.[7] The resulting sense of powerlessness may create antisocial behavior leading to violence. Powerlessness cannot accept the dictates of delayed gratification, as it interprets the lack of self-gratification as the lack of self-fulfillment.[8] Our infantile sense of weakness breeds violence, a violence bred by negative self-esteem. With such a negative self-esteem, there is no place to accept responsibility for being guilty of sin in a healthy way, Anderson contends.[9]

Such an existence of weakness is found in the early moments of separation from the womb, a time which cries for immediate attachment, as contemporary "attachment theory" has shown.[10] With a "snip of the scissors, the human infant is set adrift both physically and emotionally on the ocean of humanity."[11]

As we progress through life, our weakness is expressed in a bittersweet way in relationships with others, some joyous, some bearing the fruit of betrayal. In such a moment of betrayal by a loved one, Anderson comments, "one has become vulnerable to all."[12] Because I have "let down my guard," I have shown to others as well that I can be hurt. I am weak.

On the other hand, however, how easily I can deny my weakness! There may be good reasons to deny some traditional ideas of "Christian weakness." I surely should deny, with Bonhoeffer, the kind of Christianity that is based on making people weak, groveling in their sin, so that then the gospel can be offered to them as a solution.[13] "Religion" was a problem not a solution for Bonhoeffer and Barth. Religious people bring in God

---

6. Ibid., 73.
7. Anderson, *Self-Care*, 101–2.
8. Ibid., 105.
9. Ibid., 114.
10. Ibid., 173.
11. Ibid.
12. Ibid., 177.
13. Bonhoeffer, *Letters and Papers from Prison*, 281–82.

when their resources fail. This "God of the gaps" exploits the weaknesses of people but is thereby marginalized, since he is always on the boundaries, not at the center, of human existence.

Christian views of atonement readily speak of the vicarious *death* of Christ, and rightly so. In recent years, however, Thomas F. Torrance, James B. Torrance, and others have spoken of the importance of not just limiting the vicarious work of Christ to his death. No, from baptism to resurrection Christ lived a life for us in the entirety of our humanity. His vicarious work is a *vicarious humanity* lived for us and in our place, judging our attempts at religiosity and embracing us with a breadth and depth of love at the ontological level.[14] In this case, there is no "God of the gaps," but a God in the depths of our humanity, judging and affirming.

Certainly the reality of the vicarious humanity of Christ speaks of God displacing us in our religious "place," in order to meet us in the richness of our real existence. We may like to wallow in death and guilt, but even in that Christ intervenes. Bonhoeffer's "religionless Christianity" is an apt metaphor for the action of the vicarious humanity of Christ.

Bonhoeffer, however, can speak in another way of a genuine weakness in God. His poem, "Christians and Pagans" is a poignant testimony that the power of God is not necessarily found in simply God's availability to humanity:[15]

> Men go to God when they are sore bestead,
> Pray to him for succour, for his peace, for bread,
> For mercy, for them sick, sinning, or dead.
> All men do so, Christian and unbelieving.

Interestingly, it is "all men" that "go to God" in their distress in some way, Bonhoeffer claims, whether or not they are Christians. This is not what is distinct about Christianity.

What is distinctive is in the next stanza, where

---

14. The most important writings on the vicarious humanity of Christ are found in T. F. Torrance, *The Mediation of Christ*; "The Word of God and the Response of Man," 133–64; and James B. Torrance, "The Vicarious Humanity of Christ," 127–47. The implications of the vicarious humanity of Christ for contemporary views of salvation are discussed in Christian D. Kettler, *The Vicarious Humanity of Christ and the Reality of Salvation*. Elmer M. Colyer provides a helpful survey of the vicarious humanity of Christ in T. F. Torrance's thought in *How to Read T. F. Torrance: Understanding His Trinitarian and Scientific Theology*, 97–126. Cf. Andrew Purves, "The Christology of Thomas F. Torrance," 51–80.

15. Bonhoeffer, *Letters and Papers from Prison*, 348–49.

"For I Do Not Do the Good I Want ... and I'm Tired of Trying"

> Men go to God when he is sore bestead,
> Find him poor and scorned, without shelter or bread,
> Whelmed under weight of the wicked, the weak, the dead.
> Christians stand by God in his hour of grieving.

Here we have a suggestion of a "weakness" in God! God's weakness is seen in humanity going to God in his need. Why is he needy? Because of us, because of *our* weakness. God has become weak for our sake. This is not just a vicarious death, but also the entirety of the vicarious *humanity* of Christ. We are curiously invited to "stand by God in his hour of grieving." As the disciples were invited by Jesus to "stay awake with me" in Gethsemane (Matt 26:38), so we are invited to participate in God's "grieving."

The poem is not at an end, however, because this weakness is the weakness of the cross:

> God goes to every man when sore bestead,
> Feeds body and spirit with his bread;
> For Christians, pagans alike he hangs dead,
> And both alike forgiving.

"He hangs dead" for both the Christians and the pagans. Our weakness, our going to him in our need, has been transformed in a wondrous way by the cross. He has shared the humanity of all, Christians and pagans alike, in order to take their place in the totality of their lives, *even in their weakness*.

God does not want us to start from our strength, to affirm robustly that we are made in the image of God and redeemed by the blood of the Lamb, by the cross of Christ. The weakness of God is an indictment of our unwillingness of admit our weakness.

Are we that willing, however, to be aware of our own weakness? Pascal stops us in our tracks:

> What amazes me most is to see that everyone is not amazed at his own weakness. We behave seriously, and everyone follows his calling, not because it is really a good thing to do so, in accordance with fashion, but as if everyone knew for certain where reason and justice lie.[16]

Pascal is amazed by something. It must have been quite a feat to amaze Pascal, given his scientific genius. What is he amazed at? He is amazed at human beings, human beings who are not amazed at their own weakness, their inability, their frailty, and their finitude. Tracy, Katharine Hepburn's

---

16. Blaise Pascal, *Pensées*, 37.

character in the classic film, "The Philadelphia Story," is an attractive, intelligent Philadelphia socialite who discovers on the eve of her second marriage her own pronounced character flaw: She cannot stand weakness in others. Her inability to love others for who they are is ironically her own weakness.

In the modern world, our ideas of "weakness" can easily become an excuse to avoid moral responsibility. The Hall of Fame baseball slugger Reggie Jackson once quickly came to the defense of contemporary player Daryl Strawberry after one of Strawberry's many lapses back into drugs. "I used to think he was weak," Jackson concludes, "but now I know that it is a disease." Even if drugs and other kinds of addictions are diseases, how quickly do we moderns rush to deny any extent of moral responsibility that we are weak especially in a moral sense.

We seriously live our lives assuming that we know "reason and justice." (Is this the arrogance of Aristotle, the beginning years of western philosophy?) We very easily deny our weakness. How ironic, for it stares us in the face every day. As each day passes, I age; I gain one more fleck of grey hair . . . one more step into the grave. In the meantime, I stand puzzled about my humanity. In Pope's famous words,

> Know then thyself, presume not God to scan,
> The proper study of manhood is man.
> Plac'd on this isthmus of a middle state.
> A being darkly wise, and rudely great;
> With too much knowledge for the sceptic side,
> With too much *weakness* for the stoic's pride,
> He hangs between: in doubt to act of rest,
> In doubt to deem himself a god, or beast;
> In doubt his mind or body to prefer;
> Born but to die; and reas'ning but to err;
> Alike in ignorance, his reason such,
> Whether he thinks too little or too much.[17]

I am puzzled by myself. I have too much knowledge, so the agnostic's cynicism is not possible. But I also have too much weakness, so that I cannot possess the stoic pride of a Zeno. Even the law of God, according to Paul, can become a part of "the weak and beggarly spirits" (Gal 4:9) when it holds one captive to frustration and powerlessness (Rom 7:23).[18]

---

17. Alexander Pope, *An Essay on Man*, Ep. Ii (1733) 1.1, cited by *The Oxford Dictionary of Quotations*, 379 (emphasis mine).

18. Black, *Paul, Apostle of Weakness*, 81.

I begin by denying my weakness. I proceed to a collapse of that "character armor" (Ernest Becker) and I react. I become resigned to my weakness. I become fatalistic. I realize that I am but like the remains of Alexander the Great, the one who once conquered the known world died and became a part of the earth, the earth that now is a part of a sod house *(Hamlet)!* Hardly an honorable fate for a world conqueror let alone any person. In our weakness, we do live lives full of "the sound and the fury," and after all is said and done, they signify "nothing."

What do I hear? Who do I feel? I feel blood and flesh, the blood and flesh of Someone like me, but also unlike me. That is on Good Friday.

We thought we were sound once. Certainly that is the lie of youth. Age shows the grey and the girth all too well. "In spite of what we like to think that we are sound . . . " It is the lie of religion as well, of having "sound doctrine." Yet in spite of that, there is the flesh of Good Friday that stands before us, dripping, bloody. This bloody flesh is weakness, too. Does it have anything to do with our all too temporal flesh?

The *Via Negativa* of Weakness

"The acknowledgement of our weakness is the first step towards repairing our loss," said Thomas à Kempis.[19] I should not lie to myself. I may not be a tremendous success; there may be serious character flaws in my life. I may act like a jerk towards others. But this does not deny the importance of encouraging my self-worth. Acknowledging my weakness may paradoxically be the one of the best foundations for developing my self-worth. To lie about my accomplishments may give me a "placebo" of self-worth, but lies eventually catch up with us. There must be a better foundation for self-worth. Can it come from acknowledgement of our weakness?

I do not want to go without "ecstasy," or live in "ignorance" or "dispossession." But weakness is a kind of *via negativa*. This may be a very personal, potentially embarrassing weakness.

> But he said to me, 'My grace is sufficient for you, for power is made perfect in weakness.' So, I will boast all the more gladly of my weaknesses, so that the power of Christ may dwell in me, . . . for when I am weak, then I am strong. (2 Cor. 12:9–10)

---

19. Thomas à Kempis, cited by Castle, *The New Book of Christian Quotations*, 252.

This is the strength of the "weak" whom God has chosen in order to put the "strong" to shame (1 Cor 1:27).

I must stop at this point, though. This acknowledgement of weakness can so easily remain so much empty moral exhortation. It can easily degenerate into a demoralizing, dehumanizing self-hatred. "When I am weak, then I am strong." Paul did not say this apart from his consciousness of the vicarious humanity of Christ.

The vicarious humanity of Christ does not just present an ideal or pristine humanity, as many immediately believe when they think of the significance of the humanity of Christ. The New Testament witness often declares the sinlessness of Christ (2 Cor 5:21; 1 Pet 2:22; 3:18; 1 John 3:5; Heb 4:15; 7:26).[20] But this sinlessness is not a reality apart from his sympathy with our weaknesses: "For we do not have a high priest who is unable to sympathize with our *weaknesses,* but we have one who in every respect has been tested as we are *yet without sin*" (Heb 4:15). As Ray Anderson comments, "When we begin with a view of the self as intended by God to be free of pain and impervious to loss, we end up with a caricature of both God and human beings."[21] Who is it that God loves? Only the potential me, once I have been "cleaned up" by Christ, once I have been made presentable? No, it is the present me, warts and all. That is why Anderson rightly objects to the cliché, "We must love the sinner, but hate the sin." He remarks,

> I wonder if people who say that have any idea of how
> destructive and downright ungracious that concept is.
> Whatever my sins and failures may be, that is who I am!
> You cannot love me without accepting the whole of me,
> painful and threatening as that may be.[22]

"Unconditional acceptance" does not simply entail a moral imperative to get over one's problems, but a solidarity with the sinner. This is the legitimate *via negativa* of weakness: "For while we were still *weak* . . . Christ died for the ungodly" (Rom. 5:6). The vicarious humanity of Christ displaces our ideas of our own pristine human perfection, which we demand of ourselves in order for God to love us.

Does such a view of weakness, however, create a *necessity* for weakness, as often some view evil and suffering as a way to achieve "the greatest

---

20. Berkouwer, "The Sinlessness of Christ" in *The Person of Christ*, 239–71.
21. Anderson, *Self-Care*, 209.
22. Ibid., 218.

good"? This is common in both lay and traditional theology.[23] Was the cross really a "necessity" for God, as is commonly believed?

"God lets himself be pushed out of the world on to the cross. He is weak and powerless in the world, and that is precisely the way, the only way, in which he is with us and helps us."[24] So says Dietrich Bonhoeffer from one of the most famous letters from prison. Bonhoeffer is saying something significant about God and the cross. As Anderson observes, beginning with a self free of pain and weakness is not just a caricature of human beings but also of God. Our "caricature" of God may include a God who cannot suffer, but as such is only the traditional "working hypothesis of God" which Bonhoeffer suggests that the modern world has rightly discarded. The cross then is not a "necessity" for God, in order to achieve the greatest good or for God to be reconciled to us but instead is a demonstration of the power of God exhibited in his weakness. Indeed, is this not a greater power than shear force, a power which is able to become weak? This is "the only way" that God helps us, according to Bonhoeffer, citing Matt 8:17's quote of Isa 53:4: "He took our infirmities and bore our diseases." In Bonhoeffer's famous words, "Only the suffering God can help."[25] This is the difference between the Bible and other religions, Bonhoeffer claims. The God of the Bible is not simply the *Deus ex machina* that humanity yearns for because they have reached the end of their rope. The cross turns those aspirations of religions on their heads. There is a power here in the suffering of God. God's weakness is not the surrender of the Son to the helplessness of the Father, as Dorothee Sölle believes,[26] but it is a power we do not expect. Christ "was crucified in weakness, but lives by the power of God" (2 Cor 13:3–4). What is "sown in weakness . . . is raised in power" (1 Cor 15:43). The "weakness" of the faith of the ancient Jew Jesus, the historical figure subject to the shifting sands of historical contingency and skepticism, is nonetheless raised in power. That God provides the "religious" response in the faith and obedience of the Son is even more surprising, and threatening.

---

23. See an example in Norman L. Geisler, *Philosophy of Religion*, 376, and the self-styled Irenaean theodicy of John Hick in *Evil and the God of Love*. The essay by Ray Anderson, "Did Jesus Have To Die On the Cross?" provides a penetrating critique of the atonement as a necessary "work" of Christ, a cross without a resurrection. Anderson, *Dancing With Wolves While Feeding the Sheep*, 69–78.

24. Bonhoeffer, *Letters and Papers from Prison*, 360.

25. Ibid., 361.

26. Sölle, *Christ the Representative, an Essay in Theology After the "Death of God,"* 150; cited by Fiddes, *The Creative Suffering of God*, 2.

Paul appeals "three times" to the Lord for the "thorn in the flesh" to be removed. He did not want it.[27] But because it remains, he was able to hear from the Lord, "My grace is sufficient for you, for power is made perfect in weakness" (2 Cor 12:8–10). Acknowledging the grace of God in the midst of his weakness enables Paul to be "content with weaknesses, insults, hardships, persecutions, and calamities for the sake of Christ; for whenever I am weak, then I am strong." The "grace" sufficient for Paul is a grace of God coming into our existence in weakness, in order to be sufficient for us.

Acknowledging the *via negativa* of weakness is no compulsion upon God but similar to Socrates' teaching that the first step in knowledge is to realize that you do not know. Recognizing our weakness is such a step. There is no necessity here, but freedom, the freedom of God, the freedom of God to love, and for us to recognize that love.

What remains is the question, *How* does God's weakness help us? One answer may be found in the reality of God himself in Christ having faith for us and in our place, the vicarious humanity of Christ.

Weakness: The Inability to Believe

1) Self-Denial: Ours and Christ's

Acknowledging our weakness, as Thomas à Kempis says, can be the first step towards our restoration. But this is not the same as viewing ourselves as worthless. The vicarious humanity of Christ will not permit that. Commonly, our understanding of the process of salvation is to first feel miserable about oneself as a sinner before God and to be a failure in life and then find the grace of Christ as the solution to the problem. Experientially, that is true for many people. The vicarious humanity of Christ, however, interrupts a theology based on that experience. For such an experiential theology, as sensitive as it is to how the gospel meets human needs, can easily reinforce our sinful existence. The substitutionary atonement is not an act of Christ having to take our place because we are worthless. As Lewis Smedes puts it, we do not deserve salvation, but the very fact of

---

27. Contra Black, *Paul, Apostle of Weakness*, on 2 Cor 12:9b: "So I will boast all the more gladly of my weaknesses, so that the power of Christ may dwell in me." Black concludes, "Therefore, rather than pray for the removal of his infirmities, Paul glories in those things which reveal his weakness and utter dependence upon God" (156). If so, why would Paul pray "three times" for the "thorn" to be removed?

God's love in Christ means that we are *worthy* of salvation.[28] The longing for self-fulfillment, pleasure, and the consequent powerlessness we feel is not evil, as Ray Anderson reminds us.[29] Our desperate attempts to find that fulfillment in terms of self-gratification, particularly in the exploitation of others, are the evil. Original sin is our distorted sense of omnipotence, as bizarre as that sounds. If God has taken our place in Jesus Christ, then I do not speak the first word of my weakness. Jesus Christ and his grace speak it. As Torrance suggests, the vicarious humanity of Christ is a judgment upon our attempts to ground spirituality in either nature (Roman Catholicism) or our subjective, individual piety (Protestantism).[30] Even our weakness is not a connection to God that we can savor and nurture, to the point that God is always the answer to our need! Paul can say both "I can do all things through him who strengthens me" (Phil 4:13) and admit his weakness: "For I do not do the good I want, but the evil I do not want is what I do" (Rom 7:19). He had hope in his "deeper identity," the one who "will rescue me from this body of death" (Rom. 7:24).[31] The vicarious humanity of Christ meets our needs, also revealing both needs we never thought we had as well as our "deeper identity."

"Self-denial" is a common category in spirituality, Christian or otherwise. Calvin calls self-denial "the sum of the Christian life."[32] Self-denial, however, is radically redefined by the vicarious humanity of Christ. Christ is the One who has already *denied himself* before the Father ("yet not what I want but what you want" Matt 26:39). It is not left up for us to deny ourselves in order to reach God. If Christ has taken our place and represented us to the Father, how could we think that our attempts at self-denial would be meaningful? How would we even know what denial means? Yes, Paul can say "God chose what is low and despised in the world, things that are not, to reduce to nothing things that are" (1 Cor 1:28), but the purpose of this choice is "so that no one might boast in the presence of God" (1 Cor. 29). Not even weakness, emotional, physical, spiritual, or economic, should be praised.[33] The rug has been pulled out from under us by the vicarious humanity of Christ. Christ calls me to deny myself, but only because Christ

---

28. Smedes, *Shame and Grace*, 119f. Cf. Anderson, *Self-Care*, 161.
29. Anderson, *Self-Care*, 100–102.
30. Torrance, *Theology in Reconstruction*, 134.
31. McMinn and McMinn, "Complete Yet Inadequate," 304, 307.
32. Calvin, *Institutes*, 3.7.
33. Black, *Paul*, 99–100.

has already denied himself for me. The burden is not on my ability to deny myself! What a tortuous experience the Christian life can be otherwise! "To learn what is new we have to learn how to forget," Torrance says, "to take a step forward in discovery we have to renounce ourselves."[34] Torrance hastens to add, however, that such a radical self-renunciation is only possible in Jesus Christ, "by making us share in His life and what He has done with our human nature in Himself."[35] Thus, the life of prayer is not a mark of the *homo religiosus,* the neurotic religious person obsessed with his self-righteousness who thinks that he can coerce his way to God, gain God's approval, and proudly display his spirituality publicly (Matt 6:5,6). The prayers of Jesus were not an affirmation of the spiritual ego but a renunciation of the ego, the highest expression of trust in the Father.[36] Prayer is a kind of letting go, a release from our egos and our agendas. Prayer is admitting our weakness.

2) *The Immobility of Failure and the Faith of Christ*

Weakness is most deeply felt in failure. Whether it is moral failure, relational failure, or spiritual failure, weakness often results in failure. How can we cope with failure? Rarely do discussions of sanctification and spirituality involve a place for failure. The most terrible implication of failure is not the act of failure itself, but the results of that failure in the life of the person who failed, the legacy of betrayal, incompetence, and the lack of will power. How crushing is the loss of esteem in the eyes of friends, the public, and even in the destruction of our own ideals.

Jacob and Rachel have been crucial to the life of Mt. Zion Church.[37] Jacob has been a key part of the leadership team whose music has also contributed much to the worship team. His wife Rachel has provided leadership in Christian education. But Jacob has recently resigned from his position of leadership at the church. Jacob has just turned forty and seems to have hit the classic mid-life crisis. For years a smoldering resentment developed against Rachel. A few years ago, an opportunity to advance to a more prestigious university was halted by Rachel's refusal to move. For

---

34. T. F. Torrance, *God and Rationality,* 54.
35. Ibid.
36. Campbell, *The Nature of the Atonement,* 176.
37. This case study was provided by an anonymous graduate student in ministry at Friends University.

"FOR I DO NOT DO THE GOOD I WANT... AND I'M TIRED OF TRYING"

Rachel, the recent years of the abortion debate have rekindled guilt about the abortion which preceded the marriage to Jacob. Jacob has now entered into a relationship with a young co-worker. Nothing physical has been done yet, but he has moved out of the house.

How can Jacob deal with such an obvious moral failure? Torrance says of the vicarious humanity of Christ,

> He believed for us, was faithful for us, and remains faithful even when we fail Him, again and again...[38]

But isn't this a recipe for antinomianism? Jacob has failed his wife. Jacob has failed the church. Jacob has failed God. Even if this crisis passes, what is to keep him from finding another "sweet young thing"? And are we so far from Jacob? Don't all of us have those failures which we try to hide in our closets?

If Christ believes for us, however, if he remains faithful for us, in his vicarious humanity, does failure really have the last word? From a secular perspective, we are what our choices make us to be. We choose to be a physician or a cab driver. We choose to go to Harvard or Slippery Rock University. We choose to go to a gay bar or to a church picnic. The world will say to us, "You have your freedom, now live with your choices." In some sense, God says the same thing. Adam and Eve had their choices. And they had to live with the consequences.

Adam, however, is not the last word about humanity. The Last Adam is (1 Cor 15:48). Yes, Jacob can be morally exhorted. The result is that he is thrown back upon his own moral ability. But the mid-life crisis is too strong. The sense of failure at mid-life can only haunt Jacob.

Christ, however, has believed for us. How can Jacob believe anymore? Christ has entered into a human existence filled with centuries of failure, our fallen human nature. That is the depth of his love. "What then are we to say? Should we continue in sin in order that grace may abound?" (Rom 6:11). No, Paul responds. We have died and risen with Christ. He has taken our place. He stands before us, still believing, still trusting the Father, still possessing faith. Christ the believer, not just moral exhortation, is what will move Jacob to a repentance which penetrates to his ontological core, to the deepest recesses of his being. Even the law of God, Paul says, "weakened by the flesh" (Rom 8:3), simply reveals our moral incapacity.[39] Christ's perfect

---

38. T. F. Torrance, *Conflict and Agreement in the Church*, Vol. 2, 81–82.
39. Link, "Weakness," 995.

obedience is always before us, becoming a constant reminder and prod to become conformed to him, to be "perfect, as your heavenly Father is perfect" (Matt 5:48). Christ has already been faithful. He has not failed.

Therefore, our faithlessness, our failure, our weakness has been relativized. No longer does our faithlessness, our failure, our weakness determine our present or future. The substitutionary work of Christ, the "wonderful exchange," includes, not just the past, dying for our sins in the past, but also the present and the future as well. Jacob's failure in one sense is more terrible than he or the church believes. It is a sin against Christ, his suffering for Jacob's sake. But it is only terrible because the more glorious reality is of the one who believes and is faithful to us, incredibly, even when we are unfaithful to him.

How can Jacob's faith be restored, then? How can it be rescued, in spite of this failure? Is there a place for Jacob's faith if Christ has believed for him?

Christ's faith not only replaces the reality of Jacob's failure, but also *replaces his faith*! This is hard for us to accept. We want to hang on to our faith! Is there any place for individual responsibility then? But Jacob's failure has been replaced by the faith of Jesus. There is the loss of "the ground to do evil" when one looks at Jesus Christ, as Barth says.[40] There is an actual ontological replacement in Jacob's life because of the life of Christ. This is genuine conversion.

So Jacob's faith, too, is moved out so that he may truly believe! There is a place for Jacob to have faith, but only if it is faith devoid of any ground to stand on by itself.[41] When Jesus says, "This is my body," this has a power that does not need faith in order to give it meaning. Genuine faith can only confess the truth of Christ.[42] And this is no purely intellectualistic confession. This confession is a passionate confession, a passion that has yet to be fulfilled.[43] This passion cannot be quenched, no matter what spiritual disciplines we may fail to do, for this passion respects the faith of Christ, the one whose faith really matters. Ministry to Jacob should involve acknowledging his passion, the passion that became misdirected but should not be ignored. This is what Jesus did with the woman at the well (John 4:11–26), according to Anderson.[44] "What others may have seen as promiscuous

---

40. Barth, *CD* IV/1: 281.
41. Ibid., 243.
42. Ibid., 245.
43. Barth, *The Christian Life*, 111.
44. Anderson, *Self-Care*, 47.

sexual passion, Jesus diagnosed as an unfulfilled thirst for a love that gave back as much as it took." So, her cry, "Sir, give me this water, so that I may never be thirsty" (John 4:15) was a response to Jesus' sensitivity at the level of the physical (water, v. 7), ethnic (as a Samaritan, v. 9), and the relational (her "husbands," v. 18). He did not simply offer a pardon for sin without addressing "the restoration of the self," as Anderson puts it.[45] To do otherwise is to be guilty of religious malpractice!

Jacob's faith is "moved out" by the vicarious humanity of Christ. But it is only moved out *in order to be restored*. That is why the faith of Christ is vicarious, not just exemplary. Jesus lived a life of utter faith in and obedience to the Father, ministering in his name, teaching and healing. His healings were for the sake of empowering human beings to be truly human.[46] So when Jesus, having been touched by the sick woman, became aware that "power had gone forth from him," commends the woman for her faith (Mark 5:25–34). The vicarious faith of Jesus did not exist for himself, but for us, for our sake, in a vicarious sense, so that we too might participate in the quality of his relationship with the Father through the Spirit. This is the kind of faith which is passionate, which acknowledges the passions within us, like Jacob's, and seeks to redirect them to the Father's will. Why is it that we refuse to ascribe passion to faith? Kierkegaard cried. "Love, indeed," Kierkegaard proclaimed, "has its priests in the poets . . . but not a word is heard about faith. Who speaks to the honor of this passion?"[47]

I may wrong on large parts of my theology! I may suffer from *theological* weakness! Even Paul, however, said, "I am not aware of anything against myself, but I am not thereby acquitted. It is the Lord who judges me" (1 Cor. 4:4). My faith and my hope in time of weakness and failure are in the faith of Christ. This is faith as a "new act each day and hour" because it is in constant dependence on the grace of God.[48] Grace becomes not the excuse for easy believism but rather the constant nourishment of faith, because it is the gift of *Christ's own faith* that sustains and restores us.

Our failures and weaknesses are so devastating that just the power to overcome them is not enough. Viewing the Christian life as simply empowered by the Holy Spirit is not sufficient. The Spirit indeed "helps us in

---

45. Ibid., 9.

46. Ibid., 199.

47. Kierkegaard, *Fear and Trembling/Repetition*, 32. Cf. Rogers and Baird, *Introduction to Philosophy*, 136.

48. Ibid., 78.

our weakness" (Rom 8:26–27). This is "the Spirit of Christ" (Rom 8:9), the Spirit who enables us to participate in the life of Jesus. Christ does not simply enable us to respond. No, he acts on our behalf and in our place when our weakness is so great that we are unable to respond at all! Jacob's failure, therefore, should not be either rationalized or judged. It should be replaced ontologically by the faith of Christ.

The popular devotional story "Footprints" tells of a person looking back upon her life as footprints left in the sand. There are usually two sets of footprints, hers and the Lord's. But during her darkest days, there would be only one set of footprints. Had the Lord left her in her time of greatest need? That appeared to be the case. God seemed silent. But what was revealed to her was the exact opposite. During those times in which only one set of footprints remained, the Lord had carried her, had carried her through the valley of the shadow of death.

The vicarious humanity of Christ only takes this story one step further and deeper. When Christ is carrying us, he is also walking for us, in our place. We become like children, in utter dependence on our parents. To be like those children, Jesus said, is to enter the kingdom of God (Matt 19:14).

God does demand. But he gives what he demands.[49] This is the vicarious humanity of Christ. The Christian life is not simply the "effect" of God's demand as a "cause." That would be the result of a doctrine of God as only a sovereign, omnipotent machine. "Command what you will," says Augustine, "and give what you command."[50] The relationship between Christ and the believer is much closer than a cause and effect relationship, much closer than we ever dared to imagine. Because the Christian life is already God's project, it becomes our project, through the gift of the Holy Spirit (Rom 8:13). Otherwise, all that Jacob can say is, "Well, this was just the inevitable mid-life crisis. There is nothing I can do about it." We end up in rationalization, frustration, despair, and we eventually give up.

Jesus: The One Spirit-Led Believer

Jesus is a believer![51] How can we say such a thing? Isn't he the revelation of God, the very incarnation of God? Certainly to speak of him as a believer belittles the deity of Christ, doesn't it?

49. Barth, *CD* IV/1: 280.
50. Augustine, *Confessions*, X.29 (202).
51. Torrance, *Theology in Reconstruction*, 153–56.

"FOR I DO NOT DO THE GOOD I WANT . . . AND I'M TIRED OF TRYING"

Jesus does believe, however, as is evident throughout the Gospels. He lives a life of faith in God the Father, a life led by the Holy Spirit (Luke 4:1–14). In fact, his faith is a genuine faith, including temptations, (Matt 4:1–11; Mark 1:12–13; Luke 4: 1–13; Heb 2:18; 4:15), the struggle of Gethsemane (Mark 14:32–42; Matt 26:36–46; Luke 22:40–46), and the cry of abandonment from the cross (Matt 27:46; Heb 5:7). In Gethsemane, he counsels the disciples to "stay awake and pray that you may not come into the time of trial; the spirit indeed is willing but the flesh is weak" (Matt 26:41). Jesus knows this because it is his experience.[52] He desires the disciples' presence because "I am deeply grieved, even to death" (Matt 26:38). He invites them to share in his faith but is careful to counsel them that this is not a faith without struggle.

Instead of shying away from considering Jesus as a believer, the struggle of his believing may provide the key to the nature of *our* belief and the weakness of our unbelief. This may especially be true if we recognize that just as believers are indwelt by and led by the Spirit of God (Rom 8:9, 10, 11), so also was Jesus. Is that significant in our attempt to understand and practice the Spirit-filled Christian life? I think so. Jesus, the one Spirit-led believer, believes *before* I do. To be Spirit-led is first of all Jesus' task.

The Holy Spirit is the presence and power of Jesus Christ. The Father sends him in the name of Christ (John 14:26). It is because the Father sends the Spirit of truth to the disciples that they are not orphans (John 14:18). This Spirit will testify on the behalf of Christ (John 15:26). The Holy Spirit needs flesh. He needs the flesh of Jesus Christ. As such, Christ is repeatedly considered in the Gospels as the One confirmed and led by the Spirit (Matt 3:16; 4:1; Mark 1:10–12; Luke 4:1, 14, 18).

The Jesus who was led by the Spirit is a believer. As the Spirit is the continual presence of Christ indwelling believers, Christ must continually be believing, performing the concrete actions which characterize genuine faith, "trusting and obeying, understanding and knowing, loving and worshipping."[53] Therefore, *our* actions are not just the "results and consequences" of his action, as Thomas Smail claims.[54] In *all* of our acts Christ takes our place. He *continues* to believe through the presence and power of the Holy Spirit even today.

---

52 Martin, *Mark,* 119, 205.

53. Torrance, "The Word of God and the Response of Man," 145–46.

54. Smail, *The Giving Gift,* 109–12.

The faith of Jesus may not seem like much. In a sense it has its own "weakness." Historically, many Jewish rabbis of the first century had faith. In fact, Jesus is "the defenseless Word," in Anderson's words.[55] Nonetheless, he has *exousia*, authority, an authority which is "exposing" instead of "exploding" (Luke 4:36; 5:18–26). What his authority exposes is the judgment on our ability to judge, a judgment on our authority. As Barth remarks, his coming means our displacement.[56] We cannot truly know ourselves as sinners apart from this displacement. This is a part of his substitutionary work. "In that He takes our place it is decided what our place is." This faith with authority leads to him being sentenced for our sake throughout his vicarious life and death. His very meekness and holy love becomes an assault on our sin.[57]

This One led by the Spirit believes before we do. This is true chronologically, but it is also true theologically. His belief is the ground for our belief in order for our lives to be filled with his Spirit (Rom 8:9). "He believed for us, was faithful for us, and remains faithful even when we fail Him, again and again . . ."[58]

As the One who already believes, Jesus himself has fulfilled the two great commandments (Matt 12:28–34; Luke 10:25–28), as John McLeod Campbell observes.[59] The obedient Son loved the Father with all his heart, soul, mind, and strength, and his neighbor as himself. Jesus *already* and *continues* to love God and his neighbor. What does that mean for the Christian life? It means that the Christian life does not *need* to be lived. It has already been lived. It *continues* to be lived by the risen, exalted Christ through the Holy Spirit. He is our High Priest who represents us before the Father.

The place for the seeking of power and authority, even the power of the Holy Spirit, has already been taken. Jesus possesses it. Authoritarian Christian leaders seek for a security that ignores the vicarious humanity of Christ, the faith of Jesus.[60] Jesus has lived the perfect life of sonship.[61] In that

---

55. Anderson, "Divine Reconciliation and the Incarnation of God" lectures.
56. Barth, *CD* IV/1: 240.
57. Anderson, "Divine Reconciliation and the Incarnation of God" lectures.
58. T. F. Torrance, *Conflict and Agreement in the Church, Vol. 2*, 81–82.
59. Campbell, *The Nature of the Atonement*, 112.
60. Anderson, "Leaders Who Abuse: The Misuse of Power," *The Soul of Ministry*, 189–204.
61. Ibid., 169.

sonship there is acknowledged an abrogation of secular power, of privilege, even to the extent of death on a cross (Mark 13:32; Phil 2:6–8). The meekness of his vicarious faith became an assault on our ability to judge, our attempts at authority. Without the presence of this vicarious faith, the church degenerates into self-promotion and self-preservation. In opposition to this degeneration of the church is the authority of the kingdom of God as the presupposition of the atonement.[62] Ministry based on our own faith, and not the faith of Jesus, may proclaim pardon for sin, but only degenerate into the "religious malpractice" Anderson speaks of that does not involve the "restoration of the self."[63]

Because Someone has already believed, we now have a *source* for our faith, a source for our life in the Spirit. The Epistle to the Hebrews exhorts his readers to look to "Jesus the pioneer and perfecter of our faith" (Heb 12:2). The emphasis is upon the faith of Jesus, since he is the "pioneer and perfecter," the one who *first* has faith. The context of 12:2 makes this plain. Having just finished the roll call of the great heroes of faith in Israel (ch. 11), the author continues . . .

> Therefore, since we are surrounded by so great a cloud of witnesses, let us also lay aside every weight, and sin . . . and let us run with *perseverance* the race that is set before us, looking to Jesus the pioneer and perfecter of our faith, who for the joy that was set before him *endured* the cross. (Heb 12:1, 2).

The same Greek root word (*hypomeno*) is the root for both the *perseverance* of the Christians and the *endurance* of Jesus. There must be a connection of ideas in the author's mind, that our faith is based on the faith of Jesus, the "author of salvation" (Heb 2:10). This perseverance was based on his "hunger for an ultimate joy," as Anderson puts it.[64] "Without the hunger for an ultimate joy, He would have chosen a more accessible goal and settled for some form of immediate success." Jesus' faith was not fatalistic but had the content of hope. "Faith is a dangerous and destructive drive without hope to sustain its passion."[65]

There is an *actuality* of the faith of Jesus that dramatically and decisively creates the *possibility* of our faith.[66] Someone has already believed . . .

62. Anderson, "Divine Reconciliation and the Incarnation of God" lectures.
63. Anderson, *Self-Care*, 9.
64. Ibid., 48.
65. Ibid.
66. See the comment by Ray S. Anderson: "The actuality of knowledge of God (in

for us! Someone has already believed, in spite of our weakness. Thus our rather comical and pitiful pursuits of power and authority pale beside what God has done and is continuing to do in the midst of our weakness. This is the power and presence of the Spirit, the Spirit who indwells in and is given through Jesus.

Jesus Christ) precedes the possibility of our knowledge of God." "Theological Anthropology and the Revelation of God" lectures.

CHAPTER SEVEN

Image and Substitute

The Vicarious Humanity of Christ in a World of Genetic Engineering

"AT SOME STAGE IN the future we will have to decide how human we wish to remain..."¹ It is hard not to wince at these provocative words of the biologist Edward O. Wilson. What is to become of a Reformed theology in such a world of spectacular exhibitions of human will, with such a vast potential to mine the genetic code for breathtaking physical therapies or the possibility of a new, cloned being that we may or may not call human? Can Reformed theology with its emphasis on divine sovereignty and grace be relevant in such an audacious world filled with such *causa sui* projects? Or can Reformed theology instead bring resources to help society make decisions of life and death consequences?

The purpose of this essay is to explore the implications of a Reformed view of the image of God, based on Christ as the image of God, and particularly the doctrine of the vicarious humanity of Christ in the Scottish theologian T. F. Torrance. While it is common to speak of the atonement as the vicarious death of Christ, what if the entirety of Christ's life, death, and resurrection is atoning, lived for our sake and on our behalf? Is Jesus Christ "the perfect Eucharistic Being," in the Orthodox theologian Alexander Schmemann's words, who lives a life of thanksgiving, faith, obedience, worship, and service that becomes the basis for our lives?² Can we speak of

---

1. Wilson, *On Human Nature*, cited in Stevenson and Haberman, *Ten Theories of Human Nature*, 231.
2. Schmemann, *For the Life of the World*, 38.

the vicarious *humanity* of Christ, and, if so, would there be implications for the practice of genetic engineering?

Discussions of the *imago dei* in the history of doctrine regularly center on the question of what the image is in humanity: reason? dominion? spiritual capacity? relationality? The text of Genesis keeps us "in a certain state of suspense," von Rad wryly remarks.[3] But as Stanley Grenz has recently pointed out, the importance of Christ as the image of God in the New Testament has been grossly undervalued by most systematic theologians. "Christ is the perfect image of God" declares Calvin.[4] Paul speaks of Christ in his most exalted language as "the image of the invisible God" (Col 1:15), one of the strongest statements of Christ's deity and uniqueness yet also of his commonality with humanity. Thus, the "new self" is adopted by grace (Gal 4:4–5), "predestined to be conformed to the image of his Son" (Rom 8:29), yet not finished, in a process of "being renewed in knowledge according to the image of its creator" (Col 3:10). The lack of a christological center has often led decisions about the ethics of genetic engineering to be decided by doctrines of creation, providence, stewardship, and eschatology without a christological perspective.[5]

I will suggest four specific facets of the vicarious image of God in Christ with interesting implications for the ethics of genetic engineering: 1) Christ the unique substitute, 2) Christ the vicarious image as the Son of the Father, 3) Christ the vicarious healer, and 4) the virtue of anthropological agnosticism.

First, Christ is the unique substitute. A human clone, as controversial as that is, should be even more suspect as a moral agenda in light of its displacement by the true, unique substitute, Jesus Christ. Christ, in solidarity with humanity, affirms the uniqueness of the human that God created. The one voluntary sacrifice of Christ may give us pause concerning the involuntary sacrifice of embryos in stem cell research. The very helplessness of the embryos should remind of us the helplessness of the human clone, when that day inevitably comes. Christ's solidarity and substitution is needed to motivate the church protect what may very well be new objects of discrimination and hatred.

In the New Testament, Christ *has taken the place* of humanity in terms of the image of God, as well as the totality of our humanity. Substitutionary

---

3. von Rad, *Genesis*, 59, cited by Grenz, "Jesus as the *Imago Dei*," 622.
4. Calvin, *Institutes*, 1.15.4.
5. An example is Hui, *At the Beginning of Life*, 263, 244.

IMAGE AND SUBSTITUTE

atonement may be wider and deeper than we have thought. Not just limited to Calvin's emphasis on penal substitution, in the atonement Christ is able to do all that we cannot do. Yet he is not only the substitute. He is first of all in solidarity with humanity. There is a solidarity with the human genome (Christ as representative), but also a substitution by taking our place in our inability (Christ as substitute).[6]

Jesus is the image of God who, as the Son before the Father in triune harmony, is always before God. The miracle of grace is that he has taken our place. Yet we are faced with the increasing leaps in human autonomy as seen in bioethics. What can Christ the substitute say to these? He is a moral example, but he is also an ontological substitute, a chastening of our desire to fashion ourselves apart from God. His help, in Barth's words, is not just "from without or alongside," but "ontological . . . making their state his own," not just improving humanity but basically giving a new life and freedom, a restoration of the image of God in humanity.[7] Therefore, modern medicine cannot be a savior at the level of ontology, a tendency that is easily understood when we act as if we were not before God and physical health has become our sole concern. We may not be able to accept others, then, even our children, if they do not achieve our desires.[8] Christ as the vicarious image does not necessarily mean meticulous providence, but that the divine Word determines what it means to be human, the opposite of the temptation to be "like God" (Gen 3:5).[9]

Christ the vicarious image of God does not exclude but establishes the essential importance of the human voluntary act, something that is precluded from the clone or the embryo whose future is manipulated by others. Both are called on to sacrifice, but not with their consent.

Secondly, Christ is the Son of the Father, a trinitarian reality of belonging that is the image of God in humanity.[10] By calling God Father, Jesus has established the personal and personhood.[11] God beholds himself as in

---

6. T. F. Torrance, *Space, Time and Resurrection*, 116.

7. Barth, *CD* III/2: 212.

8. Meilander, *Bioethics: A Primer for Christians*, 44.

9. Weber, *Foundations of Dogmatics*, Vol. 1, 564; Anderson, "Humanity as Determined by the Word of God," 33–43.

10. Barth, *CD* III/2: 324.

11. T. F. Torrance, *The Christian Doctrine of God*, 16–27 and Colyer, *How to Read T. F. Torrance*, 177.

a mirror in his image in humanity according to Calvin.[12] Commenting on Calvin, Torrance claims, "Strictly speaking, there can be no image where there is no beholding."[13] The Son is "the faithful and true witness" (Rev 3:14) in humanity to the glory of God, the Son truly keeping the word of the Father.[14] The image, therefore, is not just a dead substance in humanity, but a living witness.[15]

In the persons of the Trinity we have a rich reality of personhood. The response of the Son to the Father through the Spirit is a *perichoresis,* a mutual indwelling of persons that exist in communion, not in isolation.[16] "The new man is Christ alone," declares Weber, "but not for himself alone."[17] The vicarious faithful and obedient response of the Son on humanity's behalf is the economic reflection of that immanent reality in God. But is personhood the same as humanity? Do we become persons? Can genetic engineering even facilitate that becoming? Ray Anderson suggests that there is a "middle zone" or recognition between beginnings and ends in which personhood can be "recognized."[18] Dr. Anderson was my doctoral mentor, and I am sure he would understand if I question him at this time. I try not to be an Anderson "clone" (pun intended). For Anderson, following Barth, the creature that lives and dies apart from encounter is not my humanity, but only "the undifferentiated field of the human."[19] Against Anderson, however, Calvin reminds us that in the midst of the fall's "frightful deformity" of the image, we only see the image perfectly in Christ.[20] "The world came into being through him; yet the world did not know him" (John 1:10). The "recognizable" human person may simply reflect our contemporary value of physical perfection.[21] Empirical recognition should not be the criterion for humanness.

---

12. Calvin, *Institutes,* 2.12.6. See also T. F. Torrance, *Calvin's Doctrine of Man,* 39, 42, 74.

13. T. F. Torrance, *Calvin's Doctrine of Man,* 39.

14. Ibid., 58.

15. Ibid., 71.

16. T. F. Torrance, *The Christian Doctrine of God,* 103.

17. Weber, *Foundations of Dogmatics,* Vol. 1, 578.

18. Anderson, *Dancing With Wolves While Feeding the Sheep,* 114.

19. Barth, *CD* III/2: 249; Anderson, *On Being Human,* 21.

20. Calvin, *Institutes,* 1.15.4.

21. Hui, *At the Beginning of Life,* 361.

IMAGE AND SUBSTITUTE

There is no doubt that personal identity is formed and developed. Jesus is even said to have "learned obedience" (Heb 5:8). Yet human beings struggle with their identity. Batman is not the only one who wonders whether he is truly Bruce Wayne or a costumed vigilante of the night. Will the new being be able to be a "being in encounter," able to look at another with a genuine difference, supplementing my view as "incomplete," in Barth's words, or perhaps see only a genetic reproduction?[22] Will the new being possess the joy of being with Barth's adverb, "gladly" or be like the Frankenstein monster, regretting one's own life because of alienation from others?[23]

The gospel message encounters our crisis of identities; our only hope in life and death is that we belong, body and soul, to our Lord Jesus Christ, in the famous words of the Heidelberg Catechism. We belong to God, Karl Barth proclaims. That is more important than morality and religion, because, Barth continues, Christ intercedes for the individual.[24] Intercession is for the totality of our humanity, a vicarious reality, the atonement as the development of the incarnation, in John McLeod Campbell's thought. "Covenant determination" are Otto Weber's words for this relationship, a theme resounding throughout the Reformed tradition.[25] The covenant is intercessory, vicarious, on our behalf and in our place, for all, including the defenseless, and not a Pelagian contract based on our abilities.[26] The lesson of *Jurassic Park* remains: Just because we can do something does not make it right.

The vicarious image of God in Christ is a unique expression of grace in our adoption as daughters and sons of God (Gal 4:4–5), a distinctive Reformed doctrine.[27] Barth's analogy of relations, versus an analogy of being, is helpful, as the connection of the sonship of Christ by analogy not identity to the same freedom and love that exists between the Father and the Son.[28] There is a relational connection, though not identity, therefore, with the children of our DNA, yet always critiqued by humanity as known through the Last Adam. He is "the true witness" to God, in Barth's words, in his

---

22. Barth, *CD* III/2: 255.
23. Ibid., 273.
24. Barth, *Dogmatics in Outline*, 91.
25. Weber, *Foundations of Dogmatics*, Vol. 1, 570.
26. See James B. Torrance, "Covenant or Contract?" 51–76.
27. T. F. Torrance, *The Christian Frame of Mind*, 39.
28. Barth, *CD* III/2: 220.

perfect faith and obedience to the Father, a Reformed emphasis in Christology that does not confuse the *communicatio idiomatum* (communication of properties).[29] The Son is "the perfect Eucharistic Being," in the words of the Orthodox theologian Alexander Schmemann, who in giving thanks to the Father (Matt 11:25) demonstrates the only way, according to Barth, one can affirm one's humanity: in thanksgiving.[30] An agenda to produce clones may or may not create creatures that will give thanks.

Nonetheless "the new man is Christ alone but not for himself alone." The vicarious image would include the dependent and helpless like the clone, as well as the embryo, the fetus, and the infant, and the disabled person. Our dependence on God is reflected in the dependence of the Son on the Father, a theme in both Calvin and Schleiermacher, according to B.A. Gerrish.[31]

Thirdly, Christ is the vicarious healer. Yet he is the healing before he is the healer. A Reformed theology of grace provides this caution but also a foundation for a fuller humanity under the image of God we now know in Christ. The "confused, mutilated, and disease-ridden" humanity, in Calvin's words, has already been replaced before any clone arrives on the scene.[32] Can Christ even be called "the vicarious clone" that judges all cloning?

Nonetheless, Christ continues to heal in ways that we cannot yet calls us to participate in his ongoing ministry.[33] Calvin's "frightful deformity" of the image caused by the fall is healed by Christ, setting the stage for a rigorous advocacy of genetic therapy. Humanity is a "priest of creation," as Torrance advocates, working with God to heal a groaning creation (Rom. 8:22), but not simply our cosmetic desires.[34] Jesus is healing despite our inability, in our place, on our behalf. Despite our warranted hesitancy to endorse the rampant autonomy of bioethics projects, Jesus the vicarious healer is involved in a ministry of healing as a part of his ministry of salvation. The Greek σῴζω "to save or deliver" can also mean "to heal" 16 times

---

29. Barth, *CD* IV/3. See also T. F. Torrance, "The Word of God and the Nature of Man," 105; Muller, "Communicatio idiomatum/communicatio proprietatum," *Dictionary of Latin and Greek Theological Terms*, 72.

30. Barth, *CD* III/2: 171.

31. Gerrish, *Tradition and the Modern World*. See also Hui, *At the Beginning of Life*.

32. Calvin, *Institutes*, 1.15.4.

33. Anderson, "A Theology for Ministry," 6–21, and *The Soul of Ministry*, 1–32.

34. T. F. Torrance, *The Ground and Grammar of Theology*, 1–14.

in the healings of Jesus.[35] Healing is a part of the recreation to the image by Christ the one who is the image, whose ministry of healing is unique in that he also can forgive sins (Mark 2:5). This ministry is a response to the proactive sending by the Father, the image of God as reflecting Father, Son, and Holy Spirit, including the proactive sending by the Father, as Thomas Smail suggests.[36] The vicarious response of the Son points us to the action of the Father, an action that seeks to heal. To deny the benefits of healing brought about by some forms of genetic engineering would be to deny the significance of healing in Jesus' life and ministry. In fact, one may even see some medical triumphs as the fruit of the prayers of Jesus, the high priest in the Epistle to the Hebrews who intercedes for us (Heb 10:21–22), since, according to James, "the prayer of the righteous is powerful and effective" (Jas 5:16).[37] Such prayers are an outgrowth of the mutual love between the Father and the Son in the Spirit (John 17). Still, there should be healing without exploiting the helpless.

Lastly, Christ the vicarious image speaks of the virtue of anthropological agnosticism. *Finitum non capax infiniti* (the finite cannot contain the infinite) is a time-honored Reformed dictum that reminds us of our limitations concerning knowledge of God, but also, knowledge of human beings. The pathetic curate in H.G. Wells' novel, *The War of the Worlds* laments that the Martians have been allowed to wreck such havoc on the earth despite his belief in divine protection. "What are these Martians?" he asks. His companion, the cynical narrator, simply responds, "What are we?"[38]

Anthropological agnosticism is needed since the vicarious image tells of both human creatureliness and its value. Grace neither perfects nor destroys nature but does affirm the connection between creation and covenant, as Barth stresses.[39] Grace celebrates the finitude of our creatureliness. In Barth's words, "Creatureliness can be regarded as humiliating only where the creature is thought to be in partial or total opposition to God."[40] Humanity cannot be understood apart from the Word that comes

---

35. W. Foerster, "σῴζω," 980–1012, Bromiley abridged, 1135.
36. Smail, "In the Image of the Triune God," 28.
37. See James B. Torrance, "Prayer and the Priesthood of Christ," 55–67.
38. Wells, *The War of the Worlds*, 47–48.
39. Barth, *CD* III/1: "Creation as the External Basis of the Covenant," and "The Covenant as the Internal Basis of Creation."
40. Barth, *CD* II/1: 243.

from outside of humanity, as Torrance reminds us.[41] Through Christ we understand human beings because on our own we know humanity only in its sinful state. Christ comes before Adam, in Barth's exegesis of Romans 5.[42] Our creatureliness needs to be coordinated with the other person, for that person's word or my view of her or him is incomplete without being in encounter.[43] This glad embrace of our creatureliness has a foundation in the joy that the Son has before the Father.[44] According to Luke 10:21, Jesus "rejoiced in the Holy Spirit," thanking the Father for his revelation to the "infants," not to the wise. Jesus rejoices for us and in our place. A society that is accustomed to seeking for life under our control is tempted to stretch our possibilities beyond the boundaries of God's word.[45] In addition, technology is not always successful, as postmodernism teaches us. The vicarious image of Christ is a reminder of both our lack of control and his thanksgiving of joy.

The value of human beings is not self-evident. Anthropological agnosticism recognizes that we see the value of human beings in Christ the image of God. Christ takes the place of humanity in its puzzle over its own value and therefore genetic engineering as healing is not repugnant simply because it is "unnatural." For nature to run its course can be simply fatalism without the freedom of grace. Christ represents us as the one who bears witness of his, and therefore, our value before God. "Listen to him," the one in whom I am "well pleased" said the Father on the mount of transfiguration (Matt 17:5). The value of humanity is seen in the crucified man, the one in solidarity with the little, the poor, and the sick, in stark contrast with Nietzsche's *übemensch*.[46] This is different from the project of liberal society, as Allen Verhey reminds us, which reduces the value of humanity to contractual, not covenantal, relationships. The question, "What should be decided?" ends up always trumped by the question, "Who should decide?"[47]

If we have value because of Christ the image of God, however, we must beware of assuming we can always predict the consequences of our actions. Anthropological agnosticism reminds us that our finitude includes limited

---

41. T. F. Torrance, *Theology in Reconstruction*, 102.
42. Barth, *Christ and Adam*.
43. Barth, *CD* III/2: 255.
44. Ibid., 284.
45. Hui, *At the Beginning of Life*, 363.
46. Barth, *CD* III/2: 239.
47. Verhey, "Christians and the Genome Project," 3.

knowledge, a chastening that is needed for the grandiose expectations of genetic engineering. Somatic cell therapy (for a particular person) is different from gene cell therapy, which can affect future generations in unknown ways, without their consent.[48] God in his sovereignty only knows for sure how a clone will function in society or the consequences for society because certain embryos were never allowed to live. Would a cloned child be a comfort to bereaved parents or a cruel reminder of the child that they lost? Is there not what Jean Bethke Elshtain calls a fear of "the different and the unpredictable" in the "radical sameness" of the enthusiasts for cloning?[49]

The vicarious image of God in the humanity of Jesus Christ reflects a Reformed theology that stresses the sovereignty of God with both christological indicatives and imperatives. As a critique of teleological approaches, such as Catholic and Orthodox, the eschatological nature of the vicarious humanity of Christ is neither oriented too much to the past (natural law) nor the future (theosis), without discounting past or present.[50] God has no purpose apart from Jesus Christ, the vicarious image boldly proclaims, against both natural law and an overly futurized eschatology. The image of God is found and restored totally in Jesus Christ, yet our eschatological nature is that we are predestined to be conformed to the image of God's Son (Rom 8:29). There is an eschatological exhortation that we know of only in Christ in the midst of our anthropological agnosticism. Here again is adoption by grace (Gal 4), an "unnatural" parenting. The vicarious image affects the whole of human life, and so does not leave to our autonomy the final word concerning humanity, pursuing a ministry of genuine healing in conformity to the image of the Son.[51] Only through the image of God in the Son do we have access to the Trinity, as Moltmann reminds us.[52] The concrete place of human purpose is in Jesus Christ, in the incarnation. In this place, human existence is pronounced not just as wounded but as dead, yet risen with Christ.[53] This is no ideal or obligation, or permission, Barth reminds us, but "the reality fulfilled in the person of Jesus Christ."[54] Jesus Christ, according to Barth, is "the penetrating spearhead of the will

48. Meilander, *Bioethics*, 43.
49. Elshtain, *Who Are We?* 103.
50. See also Demopoulos, "A Parallel to the Care Given the Soul," 127.
51. Weber, *Foundations of Dogmatics*, Vol. 1, 567–68.
52. Moltmann, *God in Creation*, 242.
53. Weber, *Foundations of Dogmatics*, Vol. 1, 567–68.
54. Barth, *CD* II/2: 606.

of God" that "is already fulfilled and revealed."⁵⁵ Barth's realized eschatology, as controversial as it may be, speaks boldly of the grace that has been accomplished, the perfect faith, obedience, and resurrection of Jesus, the vicarious image that has already happened.⁵⁶ Eschatology is a present reality yet not restricted to the present because we "are being transformed into the same image" by "the glory of the Lord" (2 Cor. 3:18), not a reflection of natural law.⁵⁷ Calvin stresses the image as eschatological since the image is our destiny.⁵⁸ This is the last word, not the inevitability of genetic engineering. Yet the eschatological should not be exalted at the expense of the protological or vice versa.⁵⁹ The vicarious image refuses a dualism that would allow either. A dualism upholding the superiority of God's intention in creation before redemption and consummation is not to be entertained as well.⁶⁰ The image we are to be transformed into is the same image that reflects even now the image of the invisible God (Col. 1:15).

Being in encounter characterizes our humanness, as it does for Christ, yet we realize the suffering other includes both the embryo and the Alzheimer's patient; Christ is the substitute for all. Becoming human is already present in the vicarious image. The new humanity is "Christ alone, but not for himself alone."⁶¹ He is together with us and in our place for the future, but not apart from the present.

The vicarious image, even in anthropological agnosticism, does not end, however, in despair but in joy; joy over the wonder and mystery of our humanity in the midst of our experiences of despair in that same human form.⁶² The same humanity includes the most helpless among us as well as

55. Barth, *CD* III/2: 142–43.
56. Childs, *Biblical Theology of the Old and New Testaments*, 236.
57. T. F. Torrance, *Theology in Reconstruction*, 106.
58. T. F. Torrance, *Calvin's Doctrine of Man*, 61.
59. *Contra* Wei, *At the Beginning of Life*, 158. A better perspective is offered by Verhey, "Christians and the Genome Project," 22–23: "The doctrine of the *imago Dei* has both a protological and eschatological dimension. It describes the basic constitution, and indeed the ontology of our humanity, as well as its ultimate destiny. If Adam is made in the image of God, so also is Christ, the *eschatos Adam*, the ultimate human being, who is the possibility, the actuality and the promise of a human life that images the life of God. It the first Adam shows us what we are, the last Adam promises what we shall be, and the one is the fulfillment of the other."
60. *Contra* Wei, *At the Beginning of Life*, 244, 264.
61. Weber, *Foundations of Dogmatics*, Vol. 1, 578.
62. See also Verhey, "Christians and the Genome Project," 7.

the seemingly boundless creativity given in modern medicine for healing. The vicarious image of God in Jesus Christ is the foundation for both.[63]

63. An earlier version of this essay was presented at the Reformed Theology and History section, American Academy of Religion annual conference, 2005.

CHAPTER EIGHT

Advocate and Judge

*The Vicarious Humanity of
Christ and the "Ideal" Self*

THE EMPIRICAL IS AT the heart of modern knowledge of the human being. But is there a basic problem if we use the empirical to exhaust our understanding of the human? That which is empirical about a human being, apart from brain waves and biochemistry, is the tortured person. What is the true human being: the creature that can be curious, investigating the cosmos with a sense of wonder and love, or a fearful, scared creature, vulnerable to wind, fire, and the grave, often lonely, dejected and rejected, negotiating desperately in a world he did not make? Is the latter the reality and the former a luxury? The empirical is that which Ecclesiastes observes, and leaves him to conclude nothing but "Vanity!" (Ecc 1:2). Nonetheless, even the possibility of Ecclesiastes' investigations speaks of something beyond the mundane.[1] Even the most hard-bitten positivist, addressing his "fellow carbon based bi-peds" (the science fiction author Arthur C. Clarke) can easily let his imagination run wild in science fiction such as *2001: A Space Odyssey*. And why can we write a poem?

The whole person is the object of Jesus Christ, the advocate and the judge of our humanity. No part of our humanity is hidden from the totality of the vicarious *humanity* of Christ. "The life of the self is embodied life," Anderson argues, "with the physical sphere as much a part of the self as the nonphysical (mental) sphere."[2] This includes "personal life"

---

1. Anderson, *Exploration into God*, 25.
2. Anderson, *Spiritual Caregiving as Secular Sacrament*, 38.

and "spiritual life." This is only established and reinforced by the vicarious humanity of Christ, which does not allow any aspect of our humanity to remain untouched.[3]

True humanity is not found in "faculties" like soul and body but in the perfect communion with the Father as we see in the free faith and obedience of Jesus. Christ presents the whole of his life to the Father, body and soul, dependent upon God's will. Therefore, his humanity is contingent upon a reality external to the self. Without denying the deity of Christ, the Son is to be distinguished from the Father, even to the point of a distinct will (see Gethsemane) as Maximus the Confessor (c. 580–662) argues against the Monothelites.[4] We are as dependent on God's grace in creation as we are in redemption. This we know in the relationship between the Father and the Son in the Spirit: The Son is always dependent upon the Father (John 5:19, 30; 14:31; Luke 23:46). This is the essence of his humanity.

A judge is not very welcome in our day. This kind of judge judges our perceptions of capacity as well as deep indwelt convictions about our individualism and our essential aloneness from all others. A capacity to love does not exist in an individual, but only as the Other creates it new by grace. The vicarious response of Christ, the Yes of the Son to the Father becomes our Yes - not just a word but a human movement - a healing act that we are unable to make. The paralyzed man at the pool of Bethzatha does not have anyone to put him into the pool when the water is stirred (John 5:7). It is Jesus' word, "Stand up, take up your mat and walk" that makes him well, a word from outside himself, not based on any inner capacity. As Anderson remarks, it is the Word of God that gives us "response-ability." "We are first of all grasped and known, then follows knowledge of ourselves."[5] Our genuine subjectivity is created by the creative Word of God, an orientation to the Other.

Jesus Christ is advocate as well as judge, and therefore a peculiar kind of judge. Since he has come into solidarity with all humanity in the descent of the incarnation (Phil 2:5–11), he takes upon himself all the incredible variety of human pain, from "chronic physical pain, the emotional pain of unhealed grief," to "the pain of unfulfilled desires and dreams," speaking

3. James B. Torrance, "The Vicarious Humanity of Christ," 127–47; T. F. Torrance, "The Word of God and the Response of Man," 133–64; T. F. Torrance, *The Mediation of Christ*, 73–98; Kettler, *The God Who Believes*.

4. Maximus the Confessor, "On the Two Wills of Christ in the Agony of Gethsemane," 173–76.

5. Anderson, *On Being Human*, 56.

with one voice the pain."[6] Jesus did this in weeping at the tomb of Lazarus (John 11:35). In doing so he was sharing in Mary's prior weeping (John 11:33).[7] "This is the battle of Jesus for the cause of man as God's creature ordained by God for life and not for death."[8] At this point he is creating a ministry, the ministry of the church, if the church is willing to embrace that cry of pain and cry along with the world. Words are suspect in our postmodern culture, but the cry of pain is real for all. Postmodern culture, however, is to be respected when we realize, with Anderson and Elaine Scarry that "we cannot really listen to pain, we can only share pain."[9] This movement of solidarity is the first movement in the double movement of the incarnation, and therefore, the first movement of ministry. Any other movement is not worthy of the gospel. This is where the world can begin to trust the church. There is no other way.

The Second Movement of the Incarnation: The Vicarious Humanity of Christ

There is a second movement as well, however. Jesus Christ is the one who speaks for the mute creation, who articulates the Father's love for it in the midst of and in spite of the accompanying chaos, including the *hominum confusione*. Jesus Christ makes clear that to be human is to be a "priest of creation," a patristic doctrine adopted by T. F. Torrance.[10] Christ represents creation's song of both praise (joy) and lament ("groaning") to God. He acts for creation, including humanity, doing what creation is unable to do for itself. The vicarious humanity of Christ calls us to the living presence of the person of Jesus in order to seek his mind, to create in us the sensitivity and mind of Christ.

Christ is the advocate for what is truly human. The vicarious humanity of Christ is the basis for a genuine Christian humanism that embraces and encourages human creativity and ingenuity founded on whatever is true, honorable, just, pure, pleasing, and commendable (Phil 4:8). Human beings as priests of creation can glorify God as artists and scientists (or friends or lovers) because we participate in the vicarious humanity of Christ, the one

---

6. Anderson, *Spiritual Caregiving*, 123.
7. Barth, *CD* IV/2: 227.
8. Ibid., 228.
9. Anderson, *Spiritual Caregiving*, 124.
10. T. F. Torrance, *The Ground and Grammar of Theology*, 1.

who perfectly represents humanity in trust and obedience to the Father. Is it not incredible that secular culture continues to find value in being human, and therefore, human pursuits? As Barth comments, Narcissus is alive in any age, full of "self-analysis, self-appraisal, and self-description."[11] But perhaps our age has an ironic, twisted advantage in that the youngest and oldest of our species tend to be increasingly discarded because we value only that which is productive and successful. Narcissus, however, can never know the true value of humanity: that one stands before God. Jesus Christ stands before God in his faithful humanity as advocate for his brothers and sisters. Noetically and ontologically we are not able to stand before God, though our countless idolatries, including religion, continually attempt to do so. Only Jesus Christ is able to stand before God. That is a judgment on us, but a judgment that brings good news. Jesus knows himself as addressed by God and he responds always in perfect faithfulness and obedience. While we may think that we want to be addressed by God, our lives show the opposite evidence. Addressed and known by God, Jesus Christ as our priest allows our humanity to be "radically disturbed and interrupted in the work of self-analysis by receiving the Gospel of God."[12] (Christian psychologists, take note!)

Christ is also the advocate for humanity in the church. This is particularly important as warning against the psychological unhealthiness of many in pastoral leadership (Christian pastors and theologians, take note!). In the ministry of Jesus, he reveals the deity of God but not a God who desires to be without humanity. The value of humanity may not be taken for granted, particularly if we are honest about our own misanthropy in any given day of dealing with the irritable, petty, annoying, and trivial among our fellow human beings. A radical disruption is needed to shake us out of bare toleration into the compassion of Jesus. The vicarious humanity of Christ reveals a value in humanity: God takes upon our humanity at every point to heal it and redeem it because it is human beings that are valuable to God in themselves, quite apart from their achievements and products.[13] In a technological, consumer-obsessed age, it is obvious how much of human self-image is gleaned from our reputation, the length of our resume, and the largeness of our bank account. "I produce, therefore I am!" is the new perversion of Descartes' *cogito ergo sum*. But we cannot ever produce

11. Barth, *CD* IV/3.2: 803.
12. Ibid.
13. Ibid., 799.

enough; we can never keep quite ahead of the latest technological gimmick (see Jacques Ellul on the "gadget" as that which fuels technology).[14] How easy does that kind of thinking affect the ministry of the church, when people become the means to an end rather than an end in themselves? God gives value to humanity in becoming our advocate and judge when there is no natural reason to find value in human beings. "Man is irreplaceable, however, because he is the object of the goodness of God, because he is ennobled by it, because God is his Friend and Guarantor and Brother, because God is for him, because God is his God in Jesus Christ."[15]

"God is his Friend"! How rare is it to hear those words in the history of the Christian teaching about God. The Society of Friends, the Quakers, are on target when they remember Jesus saying, "I have called you friends" (John 15:15). As friend, God takes up our case when no one else really is our friend, or wants to be our friend, when we cry in distress upon the Lord to be saved from our enemies (Ps 18:3, 6). The best lawyer may be our zealous advocate professionally but when the case is closed, our attorney is gone. Our lawyer may be obliged to only present our case in the best possible light, but not feeling obliged to admit our shortcomings. (The defense lawyer is not out for truth but to get us off!) God as friend in Jesus Christ does not simply leave us to our fate but, despite our own bad judgment, speaks for us in the vicarious advocacy of Christ while at the same time not hesitating to judge us. He is the true priest, representing his people, but he is also the priest who becomes the sacrifice. For only in coming under the judgment of God can we truly become free. This consideration of humanity is realistically governed by God's value, and God's value alone that he gives to human beings. Christ the vicarious priest is the one who listens perfectly to that verdict and accepts it into himself on our behalf and in our place. Since God became human, Bonhoeffer proclaims, we may no longer speak of God without humanity nor humanity without God.[16] That one thought is more valuable than most seminary courses I ever took.

The Judgment Upon the "Ideal" Self

The faith of Jesus intervenes, displaces, and puts to death our vain ideas and the vain ideas of others. What is shattered and destroyed? Nothing less than

14. Ellul, *The Technological Bluff*, 262.
15. Barth, *CD* IV/3.2: 800.
16. Bonhoeffer, *Ethics*, 82.

our supposed exhaustive knowledge of what it means to be human. Theologically and religiously, this is sometimes expressed as the knowledge of an original innocent Adam before the fall. This has a long history in theology, going back to early Judaism. Adam is the model of the intended reality of humanity. Augustine will build a tradition of the original innocence of Adam and leave a lasting legacy to the history of Christian thought: Adam and Eve lived in Paradise in perfect relationship with God.

> He lived in the enjoyment of God, and derived his own
> goodness from God's goodness. He lived without any
> want, and had it in his power to live like this for ever . . .
> There was no trace of decay in the body, or arising from
> the body, to bring any distress to any of his senses.
> There was no risk of disease from within or injury from
> without. Man enjoyed perfect health in the body,
> entire tranquility in the soul.[17]

Human and divine relationships were also in a state of perfection:

> But true joy flowed perpetually from God and towards
> God. There was a blaze of 'love from a pure heart, a
> good conscience, and a faith that was no pretence.'
> Between man and wife there was a faithful partnership
> based on love and mutual respect.

Apart from modern reasons for objecting to the original innocence of Adam[18] is the virtue of what we might call *anthropological agnosticism* brought about by the vicarious humanity of Christ. Even if there were an original, innocent Adam, we have no knowledge of such a human being. The only human beings we know are those who are "ungodly" (Rom 5:6), "sinners," (5:8), and "enemies" of God (5:10). The original innocence of Adam, a knowledge of pristine humanity, becomes *de facto* a non-issue. We do not know who we are in essence. We can send a satellite within a mile of Saturn, yet we remain a mystery to ourselves.[19] An idea of the original, innocent Adam seems to hide that fact. And why not? What is more terrifying that to look at yourself in the mirror and say: "I don't know who you are!" Psychologically, then, we crave and demand a pristine Adam. But theologically it simply becomes a reflection of our alienation from

---

17. Augustine, *The City of God*, 14.26.

18. Hick, *Evil and the God of Love*, 203; Pannenberg, *Anthropology in Theological Perspective*, 57.

19. Percy, *Lost in the Cosmos*, 7.

God. The vicarious humanity of Christ brings this out into the open, as painful as it is.

Is there a kind of Christian superficiality that assumes we exhaustively know what is human (along with God), but never is really grasped by the vicarious humanity of Christ? Our ideas of humanity, bourgeois or radical, remain untouched because of our refusal to admit that Christ has taken our place. Our ideas of the self continue to have destructive power. What is this power? One manifestation may be the power of *the "ideal" self*, a fantasy of our minds, of all that we *should* be.[20] For with the "ideal" self we can live without faith and, most of all, we can create our own vision of what it means to be human. We live as if we were immortal. Ultimately, of course, in one sense, we are rudely awakened at some point that this is not so. Ironically, as Kierkegaard points out, our nature as *spirit* creates the despair that one is not able to die.[21]

Human nature can be understood theologically in finding humanity's origin and goal in God, as in Dietrich Bonhoeffer's *Ethics*.[22] Jesus certainly saw his origin and goal in God. However, human nature must not be restricted to only knowledge of the origin and the goal. Bonhoeffer criticizes those who restrict God to the boundaries of life, not recognizing that, particularly in a "religionless Christianity," God will be found at the center, in the fullness of everyday life, not just restricted to "boundary events" such as baptism, marriage, and the funeral.[23] Jesus' vicarious nature was a vicarious *humanity*, the totality of his life, not just restricted to his death. Perhaps this is what Ray Anderson aims at when he describes the divine determination of humanity in terms of every area of human life: the personal, the social, the sexual, and the spiritual, and not just at the point of origin or in terms of the phenomenon of sin.[24] The vicarious humanity of Christ is a critique of our notion of an "ideal" self that may acknowledge God gladly in a "religious" way as the origin and the goal, but ignores him in the middle of human existence. Restricted to the origin and the goal, we are lost when

---

20. See Horney, *Neurosis and Mental Health*; Rogers, *Confessions of a Conservative Evangelical*, 24; Smedes, *Shame and Grace*.
21. Kierkegaard, *The Sickness Unto Death*, 24.
22. Bonhoeffer, *Ethics*, 49.
23. Bonhoeffer, *Letters and Papers from Prison*, 282.
24. Anderson, "Theological Anthropology," 89.

it comes to living a daily existence and depending upon our own "variables of self-perception."[25]

Consequences of the "Ideal" Self, Hope in the Faith of Jesus

In contrast to the vicarious humanity of Christ is our obsession with creating the "ideal" self. Why is it that the death of a celebrity becomes so significant to us?[26] What is this but the celebrity as the "ideal" self that we would like to be but which we eventually admit we can never be. The "ideal" self serves a "vicarious" function, but it is a vicariousness that is a fiction. Our celebrities can never live up to the burden we give them. Bob Dylan comments candidly on this in his autobiographical *Chronicles, Volume One*.[27] He paints a grim picture of how it feels never being able to go to lunch without knowing that someone is looking at you, whispering about you, how dehumanizing that is. Celebrities are only human with typical human desires, but we want them to be gods and goddesses. In the documentary film, *No Direction Home*, Dylan anguishes telling of his puzzlement at how, in the sixties, he was expected to the "the spokesman of the generation."[28] People were looking to him for "the answer." He had no intention or desire to any kind of spokesman, let alone messiah, and almost comically tried to distance himself by releasing albums of country western songs and old standards (including "Blue Moon"!) in "Nashville Skyline" and "Self Portrait." The cult of the tabloid newspaper in subsequent years has only reinforced that obsession. We certainly have always had heroes, but they are transformed by the "ideal" self into gods. As gods, they will eventually fail.

Communities are not always good. The community may be seen as a manifestation of the "ideal" self when it is not brought under the judgment of the vicarious humanity of Christ. Human beings are created in co-humanity, dependent upon one another, but dependence is not the same as "co-dependence," a pathological "group-think" that enslaves the individual to a particular ideology or cause (see Eric Hoffer, *The True Believer*). The vicarious humanity of Christ provides a basis, however, to be in community, but without the community called upon be its own *telos*,

---

25. Ibid., 90.
26. Anderson, *The New Age of Soul*, 89.
27. Dylan, *Chronicles, Volume One*, 121.
28. *No Direction Home*, directed by Martin Scorsese.

its own end or purpose. For Christ, having taken the place of humanity, including humanity in community, enables communities—heralded by the church as the representative of the new humanity—to have a center outside of themselves, to transcend themselves, in Langdon Gilkey's words.[29] The soul of such a community very naturally bereaves in the loss of one of its members.[30] There is nothing ideal about that. In fact, the very opposite of the "ideal" self is the self that ends in death. But will anyone notice when I die? The community will, and in the vicarious humanity of Christ, that community is not alone in its lament. Christ cries along with and for the sake of the community, as he did in Gethsemane and on Calvary. Christ represents the soul of the community for it is he who truly prays the psalms of lament, psalms that represent the whole self lamenting: "My soul thirsts for God . . . " (Ps 42:2).[31] Jesus is thirsting as the community is thirsting. We do not thirst alone. "I have a baptism with which to be baptized, and what stress I am under until it is completed!" Jesus cries (Luke 12:39). At the bottom of his soul, Jesus cries (John 12:27; Heb 5:7). His entire being, embracing our entire being, cries to the Father.[32]

Spirituality, therefore, is not found in a religious niche, but in the whole of life, where Christ has taken upon the whole of our humanity.[33] This is a stunning rebuke to the "ideal" self who does not possess this wholeness but a perverted use of fantasy that ends up condemning and betraying. The soul itself cannot be this center, as is found in many expressions of "spirituality," for it is Christ's cry to the Father, embracing the entirety of our humanity as our representative that displaces any attempt by the soul to become the "ideal" self, and thus, a false god.[34]

The vicarious humanity of Christ displaces the "ideal" self that seeks to present an ideal humanity devoid of pain: the "spiritual" self. This self also cannot deal with loss.[35] Such a view can become devastating for ministry. How can one minister to someone in deep pain or loss without acknowledging the reality of that suffering? What in effect happens is that the first movement of the incarnation, the "humanward" movement, from God to

---

29. Gilkey, *Message and Existence*, 210–11.
30. Anderson, *The New Age of Soul*, 48.
31. Ibid., 59.
32. Ibid., 91.
33. Ibid., 66.
34. Ibid., 69.
35. Anderson, *Spiritual Caregiving*, 58–60.

us, is denied, and thus ministry becomes inhuman, something that happens more often than we want to admit. In the humanward movement of God in Jesus Christ, an identification has been made with our feelings. There is much more to salvation than this, but it is not less than this solidarity. This solidarity, in fact, is the crucial first step of God, the only "preparing of the way" for the "Godward" step, the vicarious faith and obedience of Christ. This can also be a critique of spiritualities of "self-emptying" that, as Anderson astutely observes, empty the self of its humanity.[36] Barth's words are wise: If faith in its negative form is indeed an emptying, then it is certainly an emptying of all the results of such practices of self-emptying.[37]

In a nutshell, the "ideal" self does not know itself, for the "ideal" is a fiction. As Kant argues, the human mind is quite active but the activity of the mind has no necessary relation to things are they are.[38] This is also the problem with all sorts of Idealism in philosophy, from Plato to Hegel. We may have a very logical or very aesthetically pleasing worldview, logical within itself, but with one thing missing: it does not exist. In Woody Allen's comic fantasy film, *The Purple Rose of Cairo*, the despairing housewife played by Mia Farrow seeks refuge in the fantasy of the depression-era movie house.[39] One day, fantastically, the gorgeous leading man played by Jeff Bridges actually leaves the movie reality and enters into the housewife's life. She falls in love with him. Should she go back to his "movie reality" with him? She agonizes: He's got everything: he's kind, loving, good-looking, except for one thing: he does not exist. "Oh, you can't have everything!" she concludes.

The "ideal" self is a picture of how we would like to be but it has only the semblance of empty aesthetics: it is only a picture, "projected idealistically, positivistically, or existentially, scientifically or mythologically, with or without a moral purpose, pessimistically or lightheartedly, yet always with an unhealthy naivety and one-sidedness.[40]" Like the world as a whole, the "ideal" self thinks it knows itself but is simply "groping in the dark," in Barth's words. The legacy of postmodernism is a cacophony of voices proclaiming their integrity to possess their own voices but eventually all playing off against each other. The call for tolerance by the postmodern is

36. Ibid., 64.
37. Barth, *CD* IV/1: 629.
38. Kant, *Critique of Pure Reason*, 36, 128.
39. *The Purple Rose of Cairo*, directed by Woody Allen.
40. Barth, *CD* IV/3.2: 771.

assumed to be the bedrock value. But can divergent views still be maintained? Inevitably there will be the voices of protest that claim the entire enterprise of disparate voices in literature, philosophy, humanities, and the sciences must be harmonized for the sake of peace. Ray Bradbury's famous nightmare of totalitarian censorship in the future, *Fahrenheit 451,* will become the reality. Books are not only banned but set on fire by "firemen." Why? The veteran fireman exhorts the inquisitive younger man, Montag: You will inevitably become curious about what is in these books, the older man exhorts. But do not bother. They are a waste of time, being filled with contradictory ideas that tear people apart. But they must be silenced so that humanity does not waste its life in turmoil. So Montag's wife is busy with the interactive television wall of her soap opera. The "ideal" self will seek for peace at any price. But what is sacrificed is any real knowledge of the self. To know one's origin and goal may not be sufficient, but even that is missing in the world.[41] The world has no basis even to make a judgment on itself or anything else, including Jesus Christ.

The "ideal" self is constantly tempted to avoid that "lostness" by embracing a tyrannical ideal. Christ is honest enough to present us with our lostness because he is first of all the one who says, "Your sins are forgiven" (Mark 2:5). But only he can do that; it is a vicarious act. Barth's words are beautiful and to the point: "To know men is to see and understand that, as surely as Jesus Christ died and rose again for all, the grace of God has reference and is promised and addressed to all.[42]" The "ideal" self is a basic dishonesty with the self and the world: one that does not want to face how one looks in the mirror in the morning: with blurry, dark, and sagging eyes and an unkempt and unclean face. Christ acknowledges that and knows the world as it is. But he also knows that is not the whole story: "For the world as seen in all its distinctions, antitheses, and inner contradictions and yet as seen in relation to Jesus Christ and therefore originally and definitely with God, is the world as it really is."[43] What the world is, is to be caught up into the vicarious faith and obedience of Jesus Christ.

---

41. Ibid., 769.
42. Ibid., 771.
43. Ibid.

Bibliography

Allen, Woody, director. *The Purple Rose of Cairo*. Orion Pictures. 1985.
Anderson, Ray S. *Dancing with Wolves While Feeding the Sheep: Musings of a Maverick Theologian*. Huntington Beach, CA: Ray S. Anderson, 2001. Reprint: Eugene, OR: Wipf and Stock, 2002.
———. "Divine Reconciliation and the Incarnation of God." Lectures. Fuller Theological Seminary, Pasadena, CA, Winter 1981.
———. *An Emerging Theology for the Emerging Church*. Downers Grove, IL: InterVarsity, 2006.
———. *Exploration into God: Sermonic Meditations on the Book of Ecclesiastes*. Eugene, OR: Wipf and Stock, 2006.
———. *Historical Transcendence and the Reality of God*. Grand Rapids: Eerdmans, 1975.
———. "The Incarnation of God in Feminist Christology." In *Speaking the Christian God*, edited by Alvin F. Kimel, Jr., 288–312. Grand Rapids: Eerdmans, 1992.
———. *The New Age of Soul: Spiritual Wisdom for a New Millennium*. Eugene, OR: Wipf and Stock, 2001.
———. *On Being Human: Essays in Theological Anthropology*. Grand Rapids: Eerdmans, 1982.
———. *Self-Care: A Theology of Personal Empowerment and Spiritual Healing*. Wheaton, IL: Bridgepoint, 1994.
———. *The Soul of God: A Theological Memoir*. Eugene, OR: Wipf and Stock, 2004.
———. *The Soul of Ministry: Forming Leaders for God's People*. Louisville, KY: Westminster John Knox, 1997.
———. *Spiritual Caregiving as Secular Sacrament: A Practical Theology for Professional Caregivers*. London: Jessica Kingsley Publishers, 2003.
———. "Theological Anthropology." In *The Blackwell Companion to Modern Theology*, edited by Gareth Jones, 82–94. Malden, MA: Blackwell, 2004.
———. "Theological Anthropology and the Revelation of God." Lectures. Fuller Theological Seminary, Pasadena, CA, Fall 1979.
———, ed., *Theological Foundations for Ministry*. Grand Rapids: Eerdmans, 1979.
———. "A Theology for Ministry" in *Theological Foundations for Ministry*, edited by Ray S. Anderson. 6–21. Grand Rapids: Eerdmans, 1979.
Augustine, Saint. *The City of God*. Translated by Henry Betteson. London: Penguin, 1984.

———. *Confessions*. Translated by Henry Chadwick. Oxford: Oxford University Press, 1992.
Balthasar, Hans Urs von. *The Glory of the Lord. Vol. 1. Seeing the Form*. Edited by Joseph Fessio S.J., and John Riches. Translated by Erasmo-Leiva-Meirkakis. San Francisco: Ignatius, 1982.
———. *Mysterium Paschale: The Mystery of Easter*. Translated by Aidan Nichols, O.P. Edinburgh: T. & T. Clark, 1990.
Barth, Karl. *Christ and Adam: Man and Humanity in Romans 5*. Translated by T.A. Noble. New York: Macmillan, 1968.
———. *The Christian Life*. (*Church Dogmatics*. Volume IV, Part 4, Lecture Fragments.) Translated by Geoffrey W. Bromiley. Grand Rapids: Eerdmans, 1981.
———. *Church Dogmatics*. (cited as CD) Edited by T.F. Torrance and Geoffrey W. Bromiley. Translated by Geoffrey W. Bromiley, et al. 4 vols. in 14 parts. Edinburgh: T. & T. Clark, 1936–77.
———. *Dogmatics in Outline*. Translated by G.T. Thomson. New York: Philosophical Library, 1949.
———. *The Epistle to the Romans*. Translated by Edwyn C. Hoskyns. New York: Oxford University Press, 1933.
———. *The Humanity of God*. Translated by Thomas Wieser and John Newton Thomas. Atlanta: John Knox, 1960.
———. *A Karl Barth Reader*. Edited by Rolf Joachim Erler and Reiner Marquard. Translated by Geoffrey W. Bromiley. Grand Rapids: Eerdmans, 1986.
———. *Wolfgang Amadeus Mozart*. Translated by Clarence K. Pott. Grand Rapids: Eerdmans, 1986.
Begbie, Jeremy. *Voicing Creation's Praise: Towards a Theology of the Arts*. London and New York: T. & T. Clark, 1991.
Beilby, James, and Paul Eddy, eds. *The Nature of the Atonement: Four Views*. Downers Grove, IL: InterVarsity, 2006.
Berkouwer, G.C. *The Person of Christ*. Translated by John Vriend. Grand Rapids: Eerdmans, 1954.
Bernard of Clairvaux, *On the Song of Songs II*. Translated by Killian Walsh. Kalamazoo, MI: Cistercian, 1976.
Bethge, Eberhard. *Dietrich Bonhoeffer: Man of Vision, Man of Courage*. Edited by Edwin Robertson. Translated by Eric Mosbacher, et al. New York: Harper and Row, 1977.
Black, David. *Paul: Apostle of Weakness: Astheneia and Its Cognates in the Pauline Literature*. New York: Peter Lang, 1984.
Bockmuehl, Klaus. *The Unreal God of Modern Theology*. Colorado Springs: Helmers and Howard, 1988.
Bonhoeffer, Dietrich. *The Cost of Discipleship*. Translated by R.H. Fuller et al. New York: Macmillan, 1963.
———. *Creation and Fall: A Theological Exposition of Genesis 1–3*. Dietrich Bonhoeffer Works Vol. 3. Edited by Martin Rüter, Ilse Tödt, and John DeGruchy. Translated by Douglas Stephan Bax. Minneapolis: Fortress, 2004.
———. *Discipleship*. Dietrich Bonhoeffer Works Vol. 4. Edited by Martin Kuske, Ilse Tödt, Geffrey Kelly, and John D. Godsey. Translated by Barbara Green and Reinhard Krauss. Minneapolis: Fortress, 2001.

BIBLIOGRAPHY

———. *Ethics*. Dietrich Bonhoeffer Works Vol.6. Edited by Clifford Green. Translated by Reinhard Krauss, Charles C. West, and Douglas W. Stott. Minneapolis: Fortress, 2005.

———. *Ethics*. Edited by Eberhard Bethge. Translated by Neville Horton Smith. New York: Macmillan, 1955.

———. *Letters and Papers from Prison*. The Greatly Enlarged Edition. Edited by Eberhard Bethge. Translated by Reginald Fuller, et al. New York: Macmillan, 1971.

———. *Life Together*. Translated by John W. Doberstein. San Francisco: Harper and Row, 1964.

———. *Life Together/Prayerbook of the Bible: An Introduction to the Psalms*. Dietrich Bonhoeffer Works Vol. 5. Edited by Gerhard Ludwig Müller, Albrecht Schönherr, and Geffrey B. Kelly. Translated by James H. Burtness and Daniel W. Bloesch. Minneapolis: Fortress, 1996.

———. *Sanctorum Communio: A Theological Study of the Sociology of the Church*. Dietrich Bonhoeffer Works Vol. 1. Edited by Clifford J. Green. Translated by Reinhard Strauss and Nancy Lukens. Minneapolis: Fortress, 1998.

Bourchard, Larry D. "Culture." In *Handbook of Christian Theology*, edited by Donald W. Musser. 121–24. Nashville: Abingdon, 2003.

Bradbury, Ray. *Fahrenheit 451*. New York: Ballantine, 1953.

———. *They Have Not Seen the Stars: The Collected Poetry of Ray Bradbury*. Steath, 2002.

———. *The Toynbee Convector*. New York: Bantam, 1988.

Buber, Martin. *I and Thou*. Translated by Walter Kaufmann. New York: Charles Scribner's Sons, 1970.

Bromiley, Geoffrey W., ed. *Theological Dictionary of the New Testament. Abridged in One Volume*. Grand Rapids: Eerdmans, 1985.

Bultmann, Rudolf. "ζάω." *Theological Dictionary of the New Testament*, edited by G. Kittel and G. Friedrich. Translated by Geoffrey W. Bromiley. Vol. 2. 832–43, 849–51, 855–75. Grand Rapids, Eerdmans, 1964.

Calvin, John. *The Epistles of Paul the Apostle to the Hebrews and the First and Second Epistles of St. Peter*. Edited by David W. Torrance and T.F. Torrance. Translated by William B. Johnston. Edinburgh: Oliver and Boyd, 1963.

———. *A Harmony of the Gospels: Matthew, Mark and Luke, I*. Edited by David W. Torrance and T.F. Torrance. Translated by A.W. Morrison. Grand Rapids: Eerdmans, 1972.

———. *Institutes of the Christian Religion*. Edited by John T. McNeill. Translated by Ford L. Battles. Library of Christian Classics 20 and 21. Philadelphia: Westminster, 1960.

Campbell, John McLeod. *The Nature of the Atonement*. Edinburgh and Grand Rapids: Handsel and Eerdmans, 1996.

Castle, Tony, ed. *The New Book of Christian Quotations*. New York: Crossroad, 1982.

Chan, Simon. "Stopping the Cultural Drift," *Christianity Today*, November (2006) 67–69.

Childs, Brevard S. *Biblical Theology of the Old and New Testaments*. Minneapolis: Fortress, 1992.

Clément, Oliver. *The Roots of Christian Mysticism: Texts from the Patristic Era and Commentary*. Translated by Theodore Berkeley, O.C.S.O. and Jeremy Hummerstone. Hyde Park, NY: New City, 1993.

Colyer, Elmer M. *How to Read T.F. Torrance: Understanding His Trinitarian and Scientific Theology*. Downers Grove, IL: InterVarsity, 2001.

Cooper, Merian C., and Ernest Schoedsack, directors. *King Kong*. RKO Pictures, 1933.

Davies, W.D., and Dale C. Allison, Jr. *A Critical and Exegetical Commentary on the Gospel According to Saint Matthew.* Vol. 1. Edinburgh: T. & T. Clark, 1988.

Demopoulos, Demetri, "A Parallel to the Care Given to the Soul: An Orthodox View of Cloning and Related Technologies" in *Beyond Cloning,* edited by Ronald Cole-Turner, 124–36. Harrisburg, PA: Trinity Press International, 2001.

Dylan, Bob. *Chronicles: Volume One.* New York: Simon and Schuster, 2004.

Dyrness, William. *The Earth is God's: A Theology of American Culture.* Eugene, OR: Wipf and Stock, 1997.

———. *Visual Faith.* Grand Rapids: Baker, 2002.

Ehrman, Bart D., ed. *The Apostolic Fathers.* Vol. 2. Cambridge, MA: Harvard University Press, 2003.

Ellul, Jacques. *The Humiliation of the Word.* Translated by Joyce Main Hanks. Grand Rapids: Eerdmans, 1985.

———. *The Technological Bluff.* Translated by Geoffrey W. Bromiley. Grand Rapids: Eerdmans, 1990.

Elshtain, Jean Bethke. *Who Are We? Critical Reflections and Hopeful Possibilities.* Grand Rapids: Eerdmans, 2004.

Eskridge, Larry. *God's Forever Family: The Jesus Movement in America.* Oxford: Oxford University Press, 2013.

Ferguson, David A.S. *The Cosmos and the Creator: An Introduction to the Theology of Creation.* London: SPCK, 1998.

Fiddes, Paul. *The Creative Suffering of God.* Oxford: Clarendon Press, 1988.

Flannery, Austin, O.P., ed. *Vatican Council II: The Conciliar and Post Conciliar Documents.* Northport, NY: Costello, 1975.

Forster, W. "σῴζω." *Theological Dictionary of the New Testament,* edited by G. Kittel and G. Friedrich. Vol. 7. Translated by Geoffrey W. Bromiley, 965–1023. Grand Rapids: Eerdmans, 1971.

Geertz, Clifford, *Interpretation of Culture.* New York: Basic Books, 1973.

Gerrish, B. A. *Tradition and the Modern World: Reformed Theology in the Nineteenth Century.* Chicago: University of Chicago Press, 1978.

Gilkey, Langdon. *Message and Existence: An Introduction to Christian Theology.* Minneapolis: The Seabury Press, 1979.

Grenz, Stanley. "Culture: Theology's Contemporary Context," in *Essentials of Christian Theology,* edited by William Placher. 31–33. Louisville, KY: Westminster/John Knox, 2003.

———. "Jesus as the *Imago Dei*: Image-of-God Christology and the Non-Linearity of Theology." *Journal of the Evangelical Theological Society* 47, no. 4 (December, 2004) 617–28.

Gunton, Colin E. *Christ and Creation.* Carlisle: Paternoster and Grand Rapids: Eerdmans, 1992.

———. "The Doctrine of Creation." In *The Cambridge Companion to Christian Doctrine,* edited by Colin E. Gunton. 148–57. Cambridge: Cambridge University Press, 1997.

———. *The Triune Creator: An Historical and Systematic Study.* Grand Rapids: Eerdmans, 1998.

Hall, Douglas John. *Imaging God: Dominion as Stewardship.* Grand Rapids: Eerdmans, 1986.

Hart, David Bentley. *The Beauty of the Infinite: The Aesthetics of Christian Truth.* Grand Rapids: Eerdmans, 2004.

BIBLIOGRAPHY

Hick, John. *Evil and the God of Love.* Revised Edition. San Francisco: Harper and Row, 1977.

Hilary of Poitiers, *On the Trinity.* A Select Library of Nicene and Post-Nicene Fathers. Second Series. Edited by Philip Schaff, Henry Wace, and W. Sanday. Translated by E.W. Watson and L. Pullan. Grand Rapids: Eerdmans. Reprint, 1976.

Heppe, Heinrich. *Reformed Dogmatics: Set Out and Illustrated from the Sources.* Translated by G. T. Thomson. Grand Rapids: Baker, 1978.

Hoffer, Eric. *The True Believer: Thoughts on the Nature of Mass Movements.* New York: Time, Inc., 1963.

Horney, Karen. *Neurosis and Mental Health.* New York: Norton, 1950.

Hui, Edwin. *At the Beginning of Life: Dilemmas in Theological Bioethics.* Downers Grove, IL: InterVarsity, 2002.

Jüngel, Eberhard. *God as the Mystery of the World.* Translated by Darrell L. Guder. Grand Rapids: Eerdmans, 1983.

Jungmann, Josef A. *The Place of Christ in Liturgical Prayer.* Collegeville, MN: The Liturgical Press, 1989.

Kant, Immanuel. *Critique of Pure Reason.* Translated by F. Max Müller. Garden City, NY: Anchor Books, 1966.

Kehm, George. "Priest of Creation." *Horizons in Biblical Theology* 14 (December, 1992) 129–42.

Kettler, Christian D. *The God Who Believes: Faith, Doubt, and the Vicarious Humanity of Christ.* Eugene, OR: Cascade Books, 2005.

———. *The Vicarious Humanity of Christ and the Reality of Salvation.* Lanham, MD: University Press of America, 1991.

———. "The Vicarious Repentance of Christ in the Theology of John McLeod Campbell and R.C. Moberly." *Scottish Journal of Theology* 38 (1986) 529–43.

Kierkegaard, Søren. *Fear and Trembling.* Translated by Howard V. Hong and Edna H. Hong. Princeton: Princeton University Press, 1983.

———. *The Sickness Unto Death.* Edited and translated by Howard V. and Edna H. Hong. Princeton: Princeton University Press, 1980.

Kjetsaa, Geir. *Fyodor Dostoevsky: A Writer's Life.* Translated by Siri Hustvedt and David McDuff. New York: Viking, 1987.

Leith, John H. *The Reformed Imperative: What the Church Can Say That No One Else Can Say.* Philadelphia: Westminster, 1988.

Lewis, Alan E. *Between Cross and Resurrection: A Theology of Holy Saturday.* Grand Rapids: Eerdmans, 2001.

Lewis, C. S. *An Experiment in Criticism.* Cambridge: Cambridge University Press, 1961.

———. *The Weight of Glory.* Grand Rapids: Eerdmans, 1965.

Link, H.-G.. "Weakness." In *The New International Dictionary of New Testament Theology,* edited by Colin Brown, Vol. 3, 993–96. Grand Rapids: Zondervan, 1978.

Louth, Andrew. "The Cosmic Vision of Maximus the Confessor." In *In Whom We Live and Move and Have Our Being: Panentheistic Reflections on God's Presence in a Scientific World,* edited by Philip Clayton and Arthur Peacocke. 157–68. Grand Rapids: Eerdmans, 2004.

McGrath, Alister E. *T.F. Torrance: An Intellectual Biography.* Edinburgh: T.& T. Clark, 1999.

BIBLIOGRAPHY

McMinn, Mark R., and McMinn, Gordon R. "Complete Yet Inadequate: The Role of Learned Helplessness and Self-Attribution from the Writings of Paul." *Journal of Psychology and Theology* 11, no. 4 (Winter, 1983) 303–10.

Macmurray, John. *Persons in Relation*. Atlantic Highlands, NJ: Humanities, 1991.

———. *The Self as Agent*. London: Faber and Faber, 1957.

Martin, Ralph P. *Mark: Evangelist and Theologian*. Grand Rapids: Zondervan, 1972.

Matthews, Charles T. "Culture." In *The Blackwell Companion to Modern Theology*, edited by Gareth Jones. 47–64. Malden, MA: Blackwell, 2004.

Maximus the Confessor. *Maximus the Confessor: Selected Writings*. Edited by George C. Berthold. Revised Edition. Classics of Western Spirituality. New York: Paulist, 1985.

———. "On the Two Wills of Christ in the Agony of Gethsemane." In *On the Cosmic Mystery of Jesus Christ*. Crestwood, NY: St. Vladimir's Seminary Press, 2003.

Meilander, Gilbert. *Bioethics: A Primer for Christians*. Grand Rapids: Eerdmans, 2005.

Mitchell, Louis J. *Jonathan Edwards on the Experience of Beauty*. Princeton: Princeton Theological Seminary, 2003.

Moberly, R.W. *Atonement and Personality*. London: Murray, 1971.

Moltmann, Jürgen. *God in Creation*. Minneapolis: Fortress, 1992.

Molnar, Paul. *Thomas F. Torrance: Theologian of the Trinity*. Burlington, VT: Ashgate, 2009.

Muggeridge, Malcolm. *Something Beautiful for God*. New York: Harper and Row, 1971.

Muller, Richard. *Dictionary of Latin and Greek Theological Terms*. Grand Rapids: Eerdmans, 1985.

Niebuhr, H. Richard. *Christ and Culture*. Reprint. San Francisco: Harper San Francisco, 2001 (1951).

Nyssa, Gregory. *The Life of Moses II*. In *Documents in Early Christian Thought*, edited by Maurice Wiles and Mark Santer. 12–17. Cambridge: Cambridge University Press, 1975.

O'Collins, Gerald, and Michael Keenan Jones. *Jesus Our Priest: A Christian Approach to the Priesthood of Christ*. Oxford: Oxford University Press, 2010.

Oden, Thomas D. *Pastoral Theology: Essentials of Ministry*. San Francisco: Harper and Row, 1983.

Oliver, Harold H. "The Neglect and Recovery of Nature in Twentieth Century Protestant Thought." *Journal of the American Academy of Religion* 60, no. 3 (Fall, 1992) 379–404.

Origen. *On Prayer*. In *Alexandrian Christianity*, edited and translated by John Ernest Oulton and Henry Chadwick. 180–387. Philadelphia: Westminster, 1954.

The Oxford Dictionary of Quotations. Third Edition. New York: Oxford University Press, 1980.

Palma, Robert. *Karl Barth's Theology of Culture: The Freedom of Culture for the Praise of God*. Allison Park, PA: Pickwick, 1983.

Pannenberg, Wolfhart. *Anthropology in Theological Perspective*. Translated by Matthew J. O'Connell. Philadelphia: Westminster, 1985.

Pascal, Blaise. *Pensées*. Translated by A.J. Krailsheimer. New York: Penguin, 1966.

Percy, Walker. *Lost in the Cosmos: The Las Self-Help Book*. New York: Washington Square, 1983.

Purves, Andrew. "The Christology of Thomas F. Torrance." In *The Promise of Trinitarian Theology: Theologians in Dialogue with T.F. Torrance*, edited by Elmer M. Colyer, 51–80. Lanham, MD: Rowman and Littlefield, 2001.

Rad, Gerhard von. *Genesis*. Translated by John H. Marks. Philadelphia: Westminster, 1961.

Rahner, Karl. *The Trinity*. Translated by Joseph Donceel. New York: Crossroad/Herder, 1997 (1970).

Redding, Graham. *Prayer and the Priesthood of Christ in the Reformed Tradition*. London: T. & T. Clark, 2003.

Rogers, Jack. *Confessions of a Conservative Evangelical*. Philadelphia: Westminster, 1974.

Rogers, Jack, and Forrest Baird. *Introduction to Philosophy: A Case Study Approach*. San Francisco: Harper and Row, 1981.

Santmire, H. Paul. *The Travail of Nature*. Philadelphia: Fortress, 1985.

Schmemann, Alexander. *For the Life of the World: Sacraments and Orthodoxy*. Crestwood, NY: St. Vladimir's Seminary, 1973.

Schweizer, Eduard. *The Good News According to Mark*. Translated by Donald H. Madvig. Atlanta: John Knox, 1970.

Scorcese, Martin, director. *No Direction Home*. Paramount Pictures. 2005.

Shenk, Joshua Wood. *Lincoln's Melancholy: How Depression Challenged a President and Fueled His Greatness*. Boston: Houghton Mifflin, 2005.

Smail, Thomas. *The Giving Gift: The Holy Spirit in Person:* London: Hodder and Stoughton, 1988.

———. "In the Image of the Triune God." *International Journal of Systematic Theology* 5, no. 1 (March, 2003) 22–32.

Smedes, Lewis B. *Shame and Grace: Healing the Shame We Don't Deserve*. San Francisco: Harper San Francisco/Zondervan, 1993.

Sölle, Dorothee. *Christ the Representative, an Essay in Theology After the Death of God*. Translated by D. Lewis. London: SCM, 1967.

Spicq, C. *L'Épître aux Hébreaux*. I. Paris: J. Gabolda, 1952.

Staniloae, Dumitru. *Orthodox Dogmatic Theology, The Experience of God*, Vol. 1. Brookline, MA: Holy Cross Orthodox, 1994.

Stassen, Glen H., D.M. Yeager, and John Howard Yoder. *Authentic Transformation: A New Vision of Christ and Culture*. Nashville: Abingdon, 1996.

Stevenson, Leslie, and David L. Haberman. *Ten Theories of Human Nature*. Fourth Edition. Oxford: Oxford University Press, 2004.

Swete, H.B. *The Gospel According to St. Mark*. London: Macmillan, 1905.

Tanner, Kathryn. "Jesus Christ." In *The Cambridge Companion to Christian Doctrine*, edited by Colin E. Gunton. 245–72. Cambridge: Cambridge University Press, 1997.

———. "The Religious Significance of Christian Engagement in the Culture Wars." *Theology Today* 58, no. 1 (April, 2001) 28–43.

Taylor, Vincent. *The Gospel According to St. Mark*. New York: St. Martin's, 1966.

Thiessen, Gesa, ed. *Theological Aesthetics: A Reader*. Grand Rapids: Eerdmans, 2004.

Thunberg, Lars. *Man and the Cosmos: The Vision of Maximus the Confessor*. Crestwood, NY: St. Vladimir's Seminary, 1985.

Thurneysen, Eduard. *A Theology of Pastoral Care*. Translated by Jack A. Worthington, et al. Richmond, VA: John Knox, 1962.

Tidball, Derek. *Skillful Shepards: An Introduction to Pastoral Theology*. Grand Rapids: Zondervan, 1986.

Torrance, Alan. *Persons in Communion: Trinitarian Description and Human Participation*. Edinburgh: T. & T. Clark, 1996.

Torrance, James B. "The Contribution of John McLeod Campbell to Scottish Theology." *Scottish Journal of Theology* 31 (August, 1973) 295–311.

———. "Covenant or Contract? A Study of the Theological Background of Worship in Seventeenth-Century Scotland." *Scottish Journal of Theology* 23 (Fall, 1970) 51–76.

———. "Introduction." John McLeod Campbell, *The Nature of the Atonement*. Grand Rapids: Eerdmans, 1996.

———. "The Priesthood of Jesus: A Study in the Doctrine of the Atonement." In *Essays in Christology for Karl Barth*, edited by T.H.L. Parker. 155–73. London: Lutterworth, 1956.

———. "The Vicarious Humanity of Christ." In *The Incarnation: Ecumenical Studies in the Nicene-Constantinopolitan Creed*, edited by T.F. Torrance. 127–47. Edinburgh: Handsel, 1981.

———. "The Vicarious Humanity of Christ and the Priesthood of Christ in the Theology of John Calvin." In *Calvinus Ecclesiae Doctor*, edited by W.H. Neuser, 69–84. Kampen, Netherlands: J.H. Kok, 1979.

———. *Worship, Community, and the Triune God of Grace*. Downers Grove, IL: InterVarsity, 1996.

Torrance, T. F. *Atonement: The Person and Work of Christ*. Edited by Robert T. Walker. Milton Keynes: Paternoster and Downers Grove, IL: InterVarsity, 2009.

———. *Calvin's Doctrine of Man*. Westport, CT: Greenwood, 1977.

———. "The Christian Apprehension of God the Father." In *Speaking the Christian God: The Holy Trinity and the Challenge of Feminism*, edited by Alvin F. Kimel, Jr. 120–43. Grand Rapids: Eerdmans, 1992.

———. *The Christian Doctrine of God: One Being, Three Persons*. Edinburgh: T. & T. Clark, 1996.

———. *The Christian Frame of Mind: Reason, Order, and Openness in Theology and Natural Science*. Colorado Springs: Helmers and Howard, 1989.

———. *Conflict and Agreement in the Church, Vol. II: The Ministry and the Sacraments of the Gospel*. Eugene, OR: Wipf and Stock, 1996 (1959–60).

———. *Divine and Contingent Order*. Oxford: Oxford University Press, 1981.

———. *The Doctrine of Jesus Christ*. Eugene, OR: Wipf and Stock, 2002.

———. *God and Rationality*. Oxford: Oxford University Press, 1971.

———. "The Goodness and Dignity of Man in the Christian Tradition." *Modern Theology* 4, no. 4 (July, 1988), 309–22.

———. *The Ground and Grammar of Theology*. Charlottesville, VA: University Press of Virginia, 1980.

———. *Karl Barth: An Introduction to His Early Theology, 1910–1934*. London: SCM, 1962.

———. *Karl Barth: Biblical and Evangelical Theologian*. Edinburgh: T. & T. Clark, 1990.

———. *The Mediation of Christ*. Second Edition. Colorado Springs: Helmers and Howard, 1992.

———. "My Interaction with Karl Barth." In *How Karl Barth Changed My Mind*, edited by Donald K. McKim. 52–64. Grand Rapids: Eerdmans, 1986.

———. *Reality and Evangelical Theology*. Philadelphia: Westminster, 1982.

———. *Reality and Scientific Theology*. Edinburgh: Scottish Academic, 1985.

———. *Royal Priesthood: A Theology of Ordained Ministry*. Second Edition. Edinburgh: T. & T. Clark, 1993.

———. *Scottish Theology: From John Knox to John McLeod Campbell.* Edinburgh: T. & T. Clark, 1996.
———. *Space, Time, and Resurrection.* Grand Rapids: Eerdmans, 1976.
———. *Theological Science.* Oxford: Oxford University Press, 1969.
———. *Theology in Reconciliation: Essays Towards Evangelical and Catholic Unity in East and West.* Grand Rapids: Eerdmans, 1976.
———. *Theology in Reconstruction.* Grand Rapids, Eerdmans, 1965.
———. *Transformation and Convergence in the Frame of Knowledge.* Grand Rapids: Eerdmans, 1984.
———. *The Trinitarian Faith: The Evangelical Theology of the Ancient Catholic Church.* Edinburgh: T. & T. Clark, 1988.
———. "The Word of God and the Word of Man." In *God and Rationality*, 133–64. Oxford: Oxford University Press, 1971.
Torrance, T.F., James B. Torrance, and David W. Torrance. *A Passion for Christ: The Vision That Ignites Ministry.* Edinburgh and Lenoir, PA: The Handsel Press and PLC, 1999.
Vanhoozer, Kevin, "Human Being, Individual and Social." In *The Cambridge Companion to Christian Doctrine,* edited by Colin E. Gunton, 158–88. Cambridge: Cambridge University Press, 1997.
Verhey, Allen. "Christians and the Genome Project." *Health Progress* (July-August, 2002) 12–18, 58.
Viladesau, Richard. *Theological Aesthetics: God in Imagination, Beauty, and Art.* Oxford: Oxford University Press, 1999.
Wallace, R. S. *The Atoning Death of Christ.* Westchester, IL: Crossway, 1981.
Ware, Bishop Kallistos. *The Orthodox Way.* Crestwood, NY: St. Vladimir's Seminary, 2001.
Ware, Timothy, *The Orthodox Church.* New York: Penguin Books, 1963.
Weber, Otto. *Foundations of Dogmatics,* Vol. 1. Translated by Darrell L. Guder. Grand Rapids: Eerdmans, 1994.
Webber, Robert. *Worship: Old and New.* Revised Edition. Grand Rapids: Zondervan, 1994.
Weil, Simone. *Waiting for God.* New York: Perennial Classics, 2001.
Wells, David F. *The Search for Salvation.* Downers Grove, IL: InterVarsity, 1978.
Wells, H.G. *The War of the Worlds* in *The Collector's Book of Science Fiction by H.G. Wells.* Edison, NJ: Castle Books, 1978.
Wood, Ralph. *The Comedy of Redemption.* Notre Dame: University of Notre Dame Press, 1988.
Zizioulas, John Metropolitan of Pergamon. "Man the Priest of Creation." In *Living Orthodoxy in the Modern World,* edited by Andrew Walker and Costa Carras. 178–88. Crestwood, NY: St. Vladimir's Seminary, 2009.
———. "Preserving God's Creation: Three Lectures on Theology and Ecology, III." *King's Theological Review* 13 (1990), 1–5.

Index

Aaronic blessing, 67
abortion, 83
Abraham, x, 51, 67
abuse, 4, 7, 70, 82, 83
Adam, 60, 110, 119
Adam and Eve, 95, 119
adoption by grace, 104, 107, 111
advocacy, 82
aesthetics, x, xi, 35–46, 59–60, 63, 65, 123
Allen, Woody, 123
Allison, Andrew, xii
Allison, Dale C., Jr., xii, 10n19
Allison, Emily, xi
Allison, John, xii
Allison, Kris, xii
aloneness, 115
Alzheimer's patient, the, 112
analogia entis (analogy of being), 42
analogy of relations, 43, 107
Anderson, Ray S., ix, xi, 11, 27, 48, 55–56, 65, 70, 73, 82–83, 85, 91n23, 93, 96–97, 101, 106, 114–16, 123
anthropological agnosticism, the virtue of, 109–13, 119
anthropology, theological, 25, 28, 31, 47, 63–65, 75
anthropomorphisms, 71
Anselm, 10
apologetics, 48
Aquinas, Thomas, 55, 60
Aristotle, 41, 57
Arminianism, 64
art, 40–42, 46, 63

ascending the mountain (Gregory of Nyssa), 74
Athanasius, 74, 81
atonement, x, 1–23, 25, 35–46, 101, 103
  external, 15 (*see also* Atonement, "surface")
  forensic pronouncements, 4, 8, 12
  and incarnation, 7, 107
  onternal, 9
  "invisible," 18
  as the life of God in the ministry of the church, xi, 1–23
  moral example, ix, 15, 90 (*see also* Jesus Christ, example of)
  ontological, 9, 12, 16, 23, 29, 67 (*see also* Jesus Christ, ontological substitute, ontological, not just functional)
  as offering, 57, 67
  penal substitution, ix, 4–5, 8, 10, 34, 38, 77, 105, *See also* Jesus Christ, penal substitute
  as political liberation, 10
  as representative, 14, 33, 40, 47, 61, 66, 77, 107 (*see also* Jesus Christ, as representative)
  as satisfaction, 10, 15
  as substitute (in our place), 14, 25, 29–31, 33, 40, 43, 47, 59, 61, 66, 70, 77, 87, 92, 107 (*see also* Jesus Christ, as substitute)

INDEX

atonement *(continued)*
    "surface," 9–11 (*see also* Atonement, external)
    theories of, 15, 29, 35, 39, 89
    "wonderful exchange" 73, 96 (*see also* reconciliation)
attachment theory, 85
Augustine, 60, 63, 98, 119
authority, 84, 100, 101–2
Ayatollah, 3

Bakker, Jim and Tammy, 3
Balthasar, Hans Urs von, 37, 39, 41
Barth, Karl, x, 2, 9, 12, 13, 15–16, 19, 21, 27, 31, 33, 37, 41, 43–45, 48, 50, 52, 54, 61, 67, 75, 77–78, 80, 85, 100, 106–8, 110–12, 117, 123–24
    Christocentrism, 77
baseball, 88
Batman, 107
beauty, xi, 35–46, 60
    judgment of, 40
Becker, Ernest, 13, 89
beliefs/believers, 23, 28, 96. *See also* faith
belonging, 62
Bergman, Ingrid, 43
Bernard of Clairvaux, 41
Bethge, Eberhard, 22
betrayal, 85
Bible, inspiration, 73–74
bioethics, 105–8
blood of the covenant, 72, 87
blood of the Lamb, 87
Bockmuhl, Klaus, 18
body and soul. *See* soul and body
Bonhoeffer, Dietrich, x, 22, 31, 37, 43, 85–86, 91, 118, 120
books, 124
Bradbury, Ray, 21, 66, 74, 124
Brando, Marlon, 58
Bridges, Jeff, 123
Bromiley, Geoffrey, 29
Buber, Martin, 64
Bultmann, Rudolf, 54

Calvin, John, 7n15, 15, 20, 63, 70, 73–74, 93, 104, 106, 108, 112 (*see also* Calvinism)
Calvinism, 64. *See also* John Calvin, Reformed theology and tradition, Federal Calvinism
Campbell, John McLeod, 5–7, 12, 16, 74, 100, 107
celebrities, 121
Chalcedon, Council of (451 A.D.), 31
Chalcedonian Christology, 28
Chan, Simon, 59
"character armor" (Ernest Becker), 89
Christian life, 7, 10, 93–94, 97–98, 100
Christianity, 30, 86
Christology, 24, 30, 33, 50, 68, 104, 111. *See also* Jesus Christ
Chronicles, Volume One (Bob Dylan), 121
Chrysostom, 39
Church, x, xi, 1, 4, 9, 11, 14, 17, 20, 22–23, 25, 27–28, 31–33, 35, 39, 59, 64, 79, 83, 101, 116–7. *See also* community, ecclesiology, fellowship
    as community, 121–2
    as body of Christ, xi, 1, 11, 20, 23, 59, 79, 80, 81
    and creation, 59
    as "hospice," 11
    as liturgical community, 82
    ministry of, 2–5, 15, 19–20, 116, 118,
    as missional, 59
    representations of a new humanity, 122
    as a "royal priesthood," 44
    vicarious humanity in, 21
Clarke, Arthur C., 114
clones, cloning, 103–4, 106, 108, 111
comic books, 62
cogito ergo sum, 117
communion, 33. *See also* Eucharist, Lord's Supper
community, 10–11, 27, 80, 82. *See also* Church
compassion, 12, 45, 62, 117
condemnation. *See* judgment
confession of faith, 71, 96

confession of sin, 22, 23
Constantinople, Fourth Council of (869–70 A.D.), 45
cosmology, 75, 78. See also creation, doctrine of
cosmos, 44, 72–75, 78, 81. See also creation, world
covenant, 27, 51–52, 59, 67, 72, 107. See also blood of the covenant; covenant determination; covenant of grace; Federal Calvinism
Covenant determination, 107
covenant of grace, 51–52
creatio ex nihilo (creation out of nothing), 45, 47–65, 78. See also *ex nihilo*
creation, 27, 33, 37, 42, 44, 47–65, 66, 68, 72, 75–81, 104, 116. See also cosmos, nature, world theology of nature and creation
   advocate of, 72
   beauty of, 60
   christological view of, 68
   contingency of, 16n37, 54
   cries ("groanings") of, 70, 108, 116
   distinction from God, 69–82
   doctrine of, xi, 6, 12, 30, 50, 60, 104 (*see also* cosmology)
   goodness 54, 57, 58, 60, 72
   purpose for, 60
   and redemption, 69, 112
   as vicarious act, 49
creativity, 25–26, 30–31, 33, 53, 79, 82–83, 113, 116
creatureliness, 49, 106
cross, the, xi, 9, 14, 16, 19, 38, 62, 67, 73, 81, 87, 89, 91, 99–100
cry of abandonment. See God-forsakenness
culture, xi, xi, 24–34, 59, 117
   vicarious, 30

Dallas Theological Seminary, x
David and Bathsheba, 44
Davies, W. D., 10n19
death, 12, 14–15, 51, 78, 86–87, 93, 98–100, 118, 122

deification. See *theosis*
dependent, the, 108
Descartes, Rene, 117
despair, 24, 40, 47, 53, 57, 62, 81, 98, 112, 116, 122. See also melancholy
determinism, 57, 64
deus ex machina, 91
Dexter, Bonnie, xii
disabled person, the, 108
discrimination (R. S. Anderson), 65
discipleship, x, 9
diversity, 124
doctrine, 15, 24, 44, 49, 104
dogmatics, 48
Dostoevsky, Fyodor, 46
dualism, 37, 54–55, 112
Dylan, Bob, 35, 121
Dyrness, William, 26, 30, 33–34, 77

Eastern Orthodoxy, 42, 66, 74–76, 103, 108, 111
ecclesiology, 19. See also Church
ecology, 68, 76
Edmund Stanley Library, Friends University, xii
Edwards, Jonathan, 43
Ellul, Jacques, 19, 262
Elshtain, Jean Bethke, 62, 111
embryo, the, 104, 108, 112
emotional coping, 9–10
emotions and feelings, 15, 60, 83, 115, 123
empiricism, 63, 114
emptiness, 62
enhypotasia, 70
enjoyment, 61. See also joy
Enlightenment, the, 76
entitlement, 62
Ephraem Syrus, 20
epistemology, 2, 8, 18, 42, 54. See also God, knowledge of
eschatology, xi, 104, 111–12
eternal life, 14
ethics, 65, 104

INDEX

Eucharist, 32, 32n36, 39, 61, 76, 80. *See also* communion; the Lord's Supper
    offering of thanksgiving, 80
evangelicals, 29, 35, 38, 61, 68
Eve, 70
evil, 61, 72, 93
evolution, 49
ex nihilo, 64–65, 78. *See also creatio ex nihilo* (creation out of nothing)
experience, 78
expiation, 14
external behavioral change, 9

Fahrenheit 451 (book and film; Ray Bradbury), 124
failure, immobility of, and the faith of Christ, 94–98
faith, x, 9, 20–21, 28, 35, 45, 51, 53, 55, 60, 72, 78, 96–97, 101, 116, 119, 123. *See also* Jesus Christ, faith, faithfulness of, vicarious faith of, trust of
    and sight, 43
Fall, the, 43, 106, 119
fallen human nature, 68, 95, *See also* Incarnation, fallen human nature, Jesus Christ, humanity of
fallen, the, the poor, children, and the elderly, 45
Farrow, Mia, 123
Fathers, the, 74–75
fear, 15, 93
Federal Calvinism, 78. *See also* John Calvin, Calvinism, covenant, Covenant determination
fellowship, 23. *See also* Church
fetus, the, 108
Ferguson, Diane, 23n64
Feuerbach, Ludwig, 26
finitum non capax finiti, 109
forgiveness, 5, 6, 11–15, 22, 72, 82
forgiveness for sins, x, xi, 4, 16–20, 22, 23, 36, 87, 109, 124. *See also* Jesus Christ, forgiveness of (by) sins, sins, pardon for
Frankenstein monster, 107

Franks, R. S.
frui, 62
Frye, Roland M., 8
Fuller Theological Seminary, ix, 47

Geertz, Clifford, 25, 33
genetic engineering, xi, 103–13
genetic therapy, 108
Gerrish, B. A., 108
Gibson, Mel, 41
Gilkey, Langdon, 122
globalization, 24
glory, 41, 61, 79. *See also* Jesus Christ, glory of
Gnosticism, 51, 54
God, 2, 10, 15–16, 20, 23, 25–26, 33–34, 40, 43, 49, 52–54, 56–57, 60–61, 61, 63, 76–78, 81–82, 90–91, 94, 98, 104, 107, 109, 111, 117, 119. *See also* Trinity
    acts of, 18, 54, 60
    authority of, 65
    beauty of, 36, 42
    being of, 56
    belonging between the Father and the Son, 62
    city of, 82
    contemplation (*theoria*), 45, 59
    covenant love, 47 (*see also* Covenant love, 43)
    as creator, 7, 13, 27, 58, 52
    deity of, 27, 51, 117
    delight of, 15
    as deliverer, 51–52
    dependence on, 82, 108
    desire for 56
    doctrine of, 3n8, 55–56, 98
    existence of, 13, 73
    as Father, 4, 5–9, 12, 14–17, 19, 23, 25, 33, 34, 36–38, 40, 43–44, 46, 50, 52–53, 55–58, 61–62, 64, 68–70, 72–73, 79–81, 97, 99, 100, 105–10, 115–16, 122
    fear of, 6
    freedom of, 27, 47, 51, 57–62, 80, 92, 107
    glory of, 45, 54

INDEX

goodness of, 119
help of, 91
"holy sorrow" of God the Father (John McLeod Campbell), 16
humanity of, 27
impassibility of (*see* God, suffering of)
inexhaustibility of, 78
inner life of (*see* Trinity, inner life of God)
immanence of, 18
joy (enjoyment) of, 47–65, 117
as judge, 7–8, 16–17, 86, 97\
knowledge of, 2–3, 8, 23, 44, 50, 88, 109 (*see also* epistemology)
law of, 6
life of, 9, 12, 15, 18, 23, 33, 49, 50, 73
as Lord, 92, 97
love of (for and by), 6–7, 16–17, 28–52, 56, 58, 62, 73, 90, 93, 107, 116 (*see also* God, covenant of; Jesus Christ, love of)
"maleness" of, 8
ministry of, 1
as "mother," 7
of the gaps, 86
omniscience of, 55
openness to, 26, 30–31
personhood of, 80
power of, 36, 51, 64, 91
presence of, 91, 93
providence of, 61, 65
response to, 32
revelation of, x, 1, 3–5, 8, 13, 73, 78, 98
as Son, 5, 6, 9, 43, 44, 49, 52–53, 56, 58, 62, 73, 106–10, 115
source and destiny in, 31
sovereignty of, 103, 111
spirit of God, 99 (*see also* Holy Spirit)
suffering of, 91
transcendence of, 18, 80
as Trinity (*see* Trinity)
vicarious nature of, 63
vision of, 37, 41
weakness, 91
will, the, 51, 111–12

Word, the, 13–14, 38 (*see* Jesus Christ, the Word of God)
wrath of, 6
God-forsakenness, 73, 81, 99
Gospels, the, 45, 64
Good Friday. *See* cross, the
goodness, 61, 93
grace, x, 2, 4, 8, 11, 16, 18–19, 30, 41, 43–46, 48, 51, 56, 58–59, 63, 65, 70, 72–73, 77–78, 89, 92, 95, 97, 103–5, 107–9, 112, 115, 124, *See also* Unconditional acceptance
Grant, Cary, 43
gratitude (thanksgiving), 30, 33, 35, 46, 61, 72, 76, 80, 108
Greek Fathers, 12n24, 39
Gregory of Nyssa, 45, 74
Grenz, Stanley, 25–26, 104
guilt, 4, 15, 16n41, 81, 85–86
Gunton, Colin, 55, 79

Hall, Douglas John, 69
Harnack, Adolf von, 2n5, 3
Hart, David Bentley, 37, 39, 42–43, 47, 55–57, 60, 76
hate, 15, 22
healing, 9, 11–12, 16–17, 20, 21, 71, 81, 108–9, 111, 113, 115, 117, *See also* Jesus Christ, Healer
Heidelberg Catechism, 107
hell, 14
helplessness, the helpless, 28, 104, 108–9, 112
Hepburn, Katharine, 87
hermeneutics, 73–74
Hilary of Poitiers, 8, 78
hilasterion, 72
historical theology, 29
history, 51, 55
holy love, 100
holiness, 7, 48
holy of holies, 72
holy priesthood, 81, 82
Holy Saturday, 39, 81
Holy Spirit, 5, 9, 20, 25, 31–33, 37–39, 46, 53, 55–57, 59, 62, 65–67, 71, 73, 80, 97–99, 106, 109, 110, 115

139

INDEX

Holy Spirit *(continued)*
    life in the Spirit, 101
    presence and power of Jesus Christ, 99, 102
hominum confusion, 116
homoousios, 6, 80
homosexuality, 83
hope, 15, 72, 97, 101, 121–24
hospitality, 82
hubris, 75–77, 84. *See also* sin
humanism, Christian, 116
humanity, being human, human being, 5–6, 9–10, 12–13, 15–16, 23, 25–31, 34, 38, 40, 44, 49–50, 57, 59, 61, 63, 73, 75–77, 79, 81, 86–88, 94–95, 97, 103, 106–10, 114–15, 122–24. *See also* Jesus Christ, humanity of; individual; personhood; self; sin
    autonomy, 61, 65, 105, 111 (*see also* humanity, freedom)
    as being in encounter, 112
    as co-humanity, 65
    "confused, mutilated, and disease-ridden" and a "frightful deformity" (Calvin), 106, 108
    as cosmic beings, 75
    creatureliness, 109–10, 116
    dependent on God's grace in creation as well as in redemption, 115
    destiny of, 80
    filled with the Holy Spirit, 100
    freedom, 26, 30–31, 33, 64–65, 79–80, 105, 118 (*see also* humanity, autonomy)
    friend of God, 118
    as "ideal," 90
    image of God, 53, 58, 80, 87, 103–13
    incapacity or inability of, 20, 47, 53, 57, 61–62, 66, 71, 76–78, 95, 105, 108, 115
    knowledge of, 109, 114–15, 119–20
    as macrocosmos, 75, 78
    as microcosmos, 75, 78
    mind, the, 68, 123
    new self, the, 104 (*see also* new creation, new humanity)
    priests of creation, 66, 74–76, 79, 108, 116
    response to God, 13, 32–33, 36, 45, 63–64, 68–71
    as speech agents (Vanhoozer and Hall), 69
    uniqueness of, 104
    as vicarious existence, 82
    value of, 117
hymns, 32
hypocrisy, 84

icons, iconoclasm, 36, 45
"Ideal" self, the, 114–24
idolatry, 117
"image," the, 19
incarnation, the, 9, 12–13, 16, 21, 23, 27–28, 30–32, 37, 39, 55, 57, 64–65, 73, 81, 98, 111, 115, 118. *See also* atonement and incarnation
    double movement of grace, descent and ascent: humanward and Godward, 27–32, 34, 36, 38–39, 45, 72, 116
    humanward (first) movement, 123
    second movement: the vicarious humanity of, 116–18. *See also* Jesus Christ, vicarious humanity of
incarnational, 11, 32
idealism, 123
indifference, 46
individual, individualistic, 10–11, 19, 21, 28, 64, 69, 93, 107, 115. *See also* humanity
intellectualism, 60
intelligent design, 60
intercession, 82
intolerance, 33
inwardness, 9–11
Irenaeus, 51, 76
Israel, 1, 50, 74, 101

James, William, 17
Jesus Christ, 1, 11, 15, 19–21, 24, 29, 81, 84, 92, 94, 98, 99, 104, 106–7, 110, 116, 124. *See also* Christology

INDEX

as advocate, 66
as advocate and judge, 114–24
aesthetics of, 61
as amen to God, 74
in art, 36
as apostle, 72
ascension of, 44, 46, 67, 69, 71, 74, 78, 80
authority of, 100
baptism of, 37, 69–71, 122
beauty of, 35–46
as believer, 98–102
blood of, 38, 79
our Brother, 22
compassion of. See compassion
confession of faith, 71–73
confession of sins. See Jesus Christ, "repentance"
continual offering to the Father, 57, 67, 79
as cosmic being, 75
and creation, 30, 55, 77
cries along with the community, 122
death of, 16, 39, 66, 70, 84, 96
"defenseless Word, the" (R. S. Anderson) 100
deity of, 33, 56, 98, 104, 115
delight of, 37
dependence of the Son on the Father, 108, 115
distinct will of, 115
dying and rising with, 11, 29, 34, 55, 95, 111
example of, 97, 105. See also atonement, moral example
faith, faithfulness of, 16, 33, 43, 54, 72, 92, 94–102, 118, 121, See also Jesus Christ, trust of, Jesus Christ, vicarious faith of, Jesus Christ, vicarious humanity of
faith and obedience of, 53, 56, 61, 115 (see also Jesus Christ, faith and obedience of; Jesus Christ, perfect faith, obedience, service, worship of)
faithful humanity, 117
fallen human nature (see fallen human nature)

forgiveness of (by), 14, 109 (see also forgiveness of sins)
free act of, 65
giving thanks to the Father, 108, 110
glory of, 36–37, 46 (see also glory)
grace of, 92–93 (see also grace)
healer, 55, 97, 108–9 (see also healing)
hearing of (by), 36–38, 40, 69–77
hearing, speaking, confessing, singing, praying, on behalf of creation, 74–75
high priest, 14, 33, 44, 59, 67–68, 70, 72–74, 76–82, 100, 109, 117–8
his answer becomes our answer, 72
humanity of, 14, 33, 38, 63–65, 70, 73, 79, 95, 111, 115 (see also Fallen human nature, Jesus Christ, vicarious humanity of)
identification/solidarity with humanity, 15, 27–29, 31–33, 38–40, 67–68, 71, 90, 104–5, 115, 118, 123, See also fallen human nature
image of, 25, 34, 103–113
incarnate Son of God, 4–5, 8–9, 13, 55–56, 98
intercession of, 15, 66, 74, 107, 109
Jewish, 91
joy of, 37, 76, 110
as judge, 71, 77, 118
knowledge of, 14
Lamb of God, 82
Last Adam, xi, 95, 107
"learned obedience" (Hebrews), 107
led by the Spirit, 98–102
life of, 10, 14, 16, 71, 94, 98
life and ministry, 109
life, death, and resurrection of, 3, 38–39, 46, 103
as light of life, 44
as Lord, 98
love of, 14, 62, 95, 100 (see also God, love of)
mediation of, 56–57
mediator of creation, 56o57
mind of, 116
minister in the sanctuary, 59 (see also Jesus Christ, high priest)

141

INDEX

Jesus Christ *(continued)*
  ministry of, x–xi, 1–2, 4, 17, 23, 33, 37, 59, 67, 80–81, 108, 117
  Nazareth, 8, 19, 54
  obedience of, 12, 14–15, 31, 37, 46, 50, 70–73, 91, 95, 100 (*see also* Obedience)
  offering of, 67–68, 70, 77, 79–80
  ontological substitute, 105 (*see also* Atonement, ontological)
  participation in (*see* participation)
  perfect communion with the Father, 115
  "perfect Eucharistic Being, the" (Schmemann), 30, 33, 35, 103, 108
  perfect faith, obedience, service, and worship to the Father, 25, 34–35, 37, 39, 47, 55, 57, 61, 63, 66, 69–77, 108, 112, 117 (*see also* Jesus Christ, obedience of; Jesus Christ, vicarious obedience of)
  perfect life of sonship, 100
  perfect relationship of harmony with the Father in the Spirit, 46
  Pioneer and perfecter of our faith" (Hebrews), 101
  prayers of, 33, 37, 45, 66, 70, 74, 81, 94, 109 (*see also* Jesus Christ, vicarious prayers of)
  presence of, 11, 71, 80, 116
  as priest (*see* Jesus Christ, high priest, priest of creation)
  priest of creation, xi, 66–82
  prophet, 37
  receiver of the Word of God, 56
  "repentance" of, ix, 12, 71 (*see also* Jesus Christ, vicarious repentance of)
  as representative ("for us" and "on our behalf"), 56, 77, 84, 86, 92–93, 98, 100, 103, 108, 110, 112, 116–18 (*see also* Atonement as representative)
  response to the Father, 14, 22, 29–40, 45–46, 57–62, 64, 68–71
  resurrection of, 25, 34, 44, 51, 54, 69
  revelation of God, 98
  risen and exalted, 100
  sacrifice of, 6, 70, 73, 77, 118 (*see also* sacrifice)
  sanctification of, 68
  savior, 81
  self-consciousness of, 64
  service of (by), 12, 33, 59
  self-witness of, 80
  sinlessness of, 90
  solidarity with humanity (*see* Jesus Christ, identification with humanity)
  Son of God, 5, 8, 11, 31, 34, 37, 40, 79–80, 105, 107
  Son of Man, 21
  song of, 39
  spirit of, 98
  substance, not just instrument of the atonement, 34
  as substitute ("in our place"), 25, 30–33, 38–40, 42, 77, 81, 86, 93, 95–96, 98–100, 103–13, 118 (*see also* Atonement, as substitute)
  suffering of, 14, 96
  suffering Servant, 41
  teacher, 55, 97
  thanksgiving, faith, obedience, worship, and service of, 103 (*see also* gratitude)
  trust of, 12, 14, 33, 94–95
  trusting and obeying, understanding and knowing, loving and worshipping of, 99, 117
  truth of, 96
  understanding of, 14
  union with, 67–68, 73
  uniqueness of, 104–5
  vicarious act of, 43, 124
  vicarious advocacy of, 118
  vicarious Artist, Musician, Poet, and Dancer, 40
  vicarious baptism of, 37
  vicarious beauty of, 35–46
  vicarious clone, 108
  vicarious confession of, 72
  vicarious culture of, 31, 34

INDEX

vicarious death of, 14, 24, 35, 86–87
vicarious faith of, 43, 53, 65, 97, 101
vicarious faith and obedience of, 38, 106, 124
vicarious healer, 108–9
vicarious humanity of, ix–xi, 4, 12, 14–16, 19–35, 37–39, 43, 47–124. *See also* incarnation, second movement: the vicarious humanity of Christ
vicarious image as the Son of the Father, 105–8
vicarious life of, 67
vicarious life and death of, 100
vicarious joy of, 47, 49, 60, 62–65
vicarious obedience of, 62. *See also* Jesus Christ, obedience of
vicarious priest of creation, 56, 75, 77, 79, 81–82, 118
vicarious repentance of, 37. *See also* Jesus Christ, "repentance" of
vicarious response, 109, 114. *See also* Jesus Christ, response to the Father
vicarious rest of, 58
vicarious thanksgiving of, 30
virgin birth of, 12–13, 21
vision of (by), 36–38, 40, 46, 78
as witness, 37, 45, 49–50, 49, 82, 106–7.
Word of God, the, 36, 40, 42, 54, 56, 64, 69–77
worship of (by), 12, 14, 32–33, 46, 50, 59
Jesus Movement, 32
Jolie, Angelina, 43
joy, 12, 24, 27, 47–65, 76, 101, 112, 116, 119. *See also* enjoyment
Judaism, 10n19
Judgment, condemnation, 11, 50, 78, 93, 93, 98, 100, 117–21, 124
of the vicarious humanity of Christ, 43
Jüngel, Eberhard, 16
Jurassic Park (book and film), 107
Justin Martyr, 32, 32n36
justice, 72

justification by faith, 78

Kant, Immanuel, 13, 123
Kempis, Thomas à, 89, 92,
Kierkegaard, Søren, 97
King Kong (film), 35
Kingdom of God, 98, 101
knowledge, 61

lament. *See* despair
Last Supper, 67
law, 7, 88
Lazarus, 116
Leith, John, xi, 17
Lewis, Alan E., 39, 81
Lewis, C. S., 41
liberal arts, 60
liberation, 19
life, 12, 51, 78
life and death, 103, 116
liturgy, 32, 39, 59
logos, 55. *See also* Jesus Christ, Word of God; Word (of God), the
logos asarkos, 54–55
Lone Ranger, 64
Lord's Prayer, 43, 67, 70
Lord's Supper, 73. *See also* communion; Eucharist
Love, ix, 5, 12, 16n41, 22, 25, 56–62, 65, 72, 77, 86, 97, 115, 119, 123. *See also* God, love of
holy love
inability to, as weakness, 88
as suffering love, 9
unconditional, 43
Luther, Martin, 63

Mackinnon, D. M., 83
Macmurray, John, 58, 60, 82
management skills, 17
Manichaeism, 61
Marxism, 18
Mary, 116
Matthews, Charles, 26
Maximus the Confessor, 75, 115
meaning-making, 25–26
medicine, 105, 109, 113

INDEX

marriage, 119
medieval theology, 78
meekness, 100, 101
melancholy, 53. *See also* despair
Melchizedek, 67
mercy, 6, 45, 86
mercy seat, 72
Michelangelo, 50
ministry, 17, 23 101, 111, 116. *See also* Jesus Christ, ministry of
ministry, theology of, 1–4, 19. *See also* ministry, theology
misanthropy, 117
mission, 81–82
Moberly, R. C., 12–13
Moltmann, Jürgen, 38, 111
monism, 55
Moses, 40
moral knowledge, 14
morality, 14, 79, 90, 95, 107
Moses, 67, 72
Mother Teresa, 41
Mozart, Wolfgang Amadeus, 45
music, 45
Myers, Bob, x
mysticism, pantheistic, 10
myth, 81

Narcissus, 117
Nathanael, 44
natural law, 111–12
natural theology, 30, 52, 60
nature, 77–78, 80, 93, 109. *See also* creation
Neoplatonism, 45, 55
new creation, new humanity, 31, 54–57, 112. *See also* humanity, new self
New Testament, 73
Nicaea, Council of (325 A.D.), 61
Nicene Creed, 6, 44, 48, 51, 61
Nicolas of Cusa, 60
Niebuhr, H. Richard, 26, 29, 59
No Direction Home (film), 121

Obama, Barack, 28
obedience, 46. *See also* Jesus Christ, obedience of

O'Connor, Flannery, 41
Oden, Thomas, 17
Oliver, Harold H., 77
omnipotence, 93
ontological, not just functional, 72–73, 86, 95, 98
order, 76
Origen, 70
Orthodox churches. *See* Eastern Orthodoxy
Overholt, Willis, xii

pain, 115
panentheism, 49, 57, 79–80, 82
pantheism, 49, 57, 79
paradise, 119
Parmenter, Bruce, 83n64
participation (in God, in Christ), 9, 32–33, 39, 46–47, 56, 69, 73, 75, 80–81, 87, 94, 97–98, 108, 116. *See also* God, life of
Pascal, Blaise, 87
passion, 96–97
pastors and pastoral problems, 17, 22, 47, 56, 61, 117
pastoral care, 6–7, 14, 19, 23
pathos, 62
patience, 11
patristic theology, 66, 116
Pauck, Wilhelm, 2, 9
Paul, xi, 51, 70, 79, 81, 84–85, 88, 92–93, 95, 97, 104
peace, 52
Pelagianism, 60, 107
Penal substitution, *See* Atonement, penal substitution
perfectionism, 57
perichoresis, 58, 106. *See also* Trinity
perseverance, 101
personhood, 82, 105–6. *See also* humanity
Peter, 20
Pharisees, 64
philosophy, 123
Pietism, 19, 38
piety, 93
Pitt, Brad, 43

144

Plato, 35, 41, 54, 123
pleasure, 93
Plotinus, 45
poets, poetry, 97
Polanyi, Michael, 30
politics, 17, 21
Pope, Alexander, 88
possessions, 61–62, 64
postmodernism, x, 14, 24, 27, 29, 37, 110, 116, 123
power, 61, 89, 91, 100, 102
powerlessness, 93
praise, 72, 116
prayer, 9, 33–34, 50, 70, 86, 94, 99, 109, *See also* Jesus Christ, prayers of
preaching, proclamation, 3, 3n7, 7, 15, 19–20, 23, 55, 60
predestination, 104, 111
pride. *See* hubris
priest. *See* Jesus Christ, priest of creation
priesthood, levitical, 74, 81
priests, priesthood, 77, 80–81, 84, 97
process theology, 54, 79
propitiation, 12
Protestantism, x, 43, 77, 93
protological, 112
providence, 104–5
psychology, 1, 10, 17
The Purple Rose of Cairo (film), 123
"purpose-driven life," 59–60, 63

Quakers (The Society of Friends), 118
Quinones, Michelle, xii

Rad, Gerhard von, 104
"Rahner's Rule," 57, 106. *See also* Trinity
rationalism, 64, 68, 80
recapitulation, 76–77
reconciliation, 1–5, 9, 12, 16, 16n41, 34, 44, 48, 68, 73, 76, 79, 81, 91. *See also* Atonement, "wonderful exchange"
redemption, 36–37, 44, 47–48, 53, 59–60, 69, 75, 77–78, 117
Reformed theology and tradition, 36, 57, 80, 103, 107–9, 111. *See also* Calvinism

relativism, 29
religion, 13, 25–26, 41, 63, 77, 85, 91, 107, 117
"religionless Christianity" (Bonhoeffer), 86, 120
"religious malpractice" (R. S. Anderson), 101
repentance, 95
"response-ability" (R. S. Anderson), 70, 115
revelation. *See* God, revelation of
revivalism, 22
righteousness, 48
rituals, 82
Roman Catholicism, 42, 93, 111

Sabbath, 58, 82
sacerdotalism, 20
sacrifice, 65. *See also* Jesus Christ, sacrifice of
Sadducees, 64
salvation, ix–xi, 2, 6, 10, 18, 21, 33, 60–61, 68, 78, 81, 101, 108, 123, *See also* Jesus Christ, savior
  Ontological, internal, 9, 72–73, 86, 95, 98
salvation history, 43
sanctification, 68, 94, *See also* Jesus Christ, sanctification of
Santmire, H. Paul, 77
Sarah, 47, 53, 78
Satan, 72
Scarry, Elaine, 115
Schleiermacher, Friedrich, 108
Schmemann, Alexander, 30, 35, 74, 77, 103, 108
Schweizer, Eduard, 20
science, 48–50, 76–77, 79
scientific method, 2
Scotus, John Duns, 55
Scripture, xi, 18, 51
self, the, xi, xi, 10, 97, 114–15, 123. *See also* humanity
self, the, "ideal," xi, 114–24
self-denial, 92–94
self-esteem, self-worth, 84–85, 89, 92
self-fulfillment, 93

145

INDEX

self-gratification, 93
self-image, 117
self-knowledge, 124
self-righteousness, 94
seminary, 118
service, 12
servum arbitrium, 63
sex, 65, 97
shadow, the, 44
shame, 4, 25, 83
silence, 70
sin, 2–3, 6–7, 9–15, 19, 22, 27, 38, 50, 56, 67–68, 70, 74, 85–86, 90, 92, 95–96, 100–1, 119. *See also* hubris
Sin, original, 99, 110
sin, pardon for, 101, *See also* forgiveness for sins
Smail, Thomas (Tom), 99, 109
social justice, 9, 17, 19
Socinianism, 12
solidarity, 25. *See also* Jesus Christ, identification/solidarity with humanity
Sölle, Dorothee, 91
soteriology, ix, 38, 48. *See also* salvation
soul and body, 15, 21n60, 28–29, 31, 79, 81, 107, 115
Speidell, Todd, 23n64
Spider-Man, 74
spiritual determinism, 64
spiritual formation, 9
spirituality, 93–94
Stellvertretung ("vicarious representative action" in Bonhoeffer), 63
stem-cell research, 104
Stephen, 50
stewardship, 104
stoicism, 88
substitutionary atonement. *See also* atonement, substitution; Jesus Christ, as substitute
Sullivan, Michael, xii
Superman, 44
supralapsarianism, 59
synergism, 33, 53

Tanner, Kathryn, 77–78

Taylor, Vincent, 20
teaching, 7
technology, 76, 110, 117–18
teleology, 60, 111
terror, 15
thanksgiving. *See also* gratitude; Jesus Christ, thanksgiving, faith, obedience, worship, and service of
theism, 49
theology, theologians, 1–4, 7, 16–17, 24, 28, 32, 35, 40, 45, 50, 55, 59–60, 76–77, 81, 83, 92, 97, 117, 119. *See also* Reformed theology and tradition
theology and ministry, 48
theology, "kerymatic," 18
theology of nature and creation, 68, 77–78. *See also* creation
theosis (deification), 12n24, 38, 46, 111
Thurneysen, Eduard, 13–14, 19
Tillich, Paul, 30
tolerance, 123
Tonto, 64
Torrance, James B., x–xi, 7n15, 16n41, 32, 74
Torrance, Thomas F. (T. F.), xi, 2, 7n11, 14, 16n37, 24, 30, 35, 44, 47–49, 51, 68, 72–76, 78–81, 93–94, 103, 106, 108, 110, 116
tradition, xi, 32
tragic, tragedy, 38–39, 40
Trinity, 9, 31–32, 43, 50, 55, 57, 58, 60, 66, 73, 82, 105–6, 109, 111, 115. *See also perichoresis*; "Rahner's Rule"
as the inner life of God, 9, 18, 43, 46, 48, 50–52, 62, 65
Troeltsch, Ernst, 26
true, beautiful and good, the, 35, 40, 45
2001: A Space Odyssey (book and film), 114

unconditional acceptance, 90. *See also* grace
unitary thinking, 55
universalism, 16n41
uti, 62

INDEX

Van Haren, Donna, 23n64
Vanhoozer, Kevin, 69
Verhey, Allen, 112n59
vicarious act in art and beauty, 39
vicarious existence, *See* Humanity as vicarious existence
vicarious humanity of Christ, *See* Jesus Christ, vicarious humanity of
vicarious knowledge, 42–44
vicarious language, 42
Victor of Antioch, 20
virtues, 65
vocation, 76,

war, 61
War of the Worlds, The (book), 109
Wayne, Bruce, 107
weakness, xi, 67, 83–102
Weber, Otto, 106–7

Weil, Simone, 45
Wells, H. G., 109
Wilson, Edward O., 103
witness, 28, 28n15, 34, 45. *See also* Jesus Christ, witness of
Word (of God), the, 19–20, 25, 28, 37, 51, 57–58, 60, 68, 70, 81, 109–10, 115. *See also* Jesus Christ, Word of God; God, word of
works righteousness, 2
world, the, x-xi, 1–2, 20, 46–47, 52, 66, 76, 79, 82, 91, 106, 116, 123. *See also* creation, cosmos
worldview, 29, 53–54, 76, 123
worship, 35, 45–46, 72. *See also* Jesus Christ, worship of (by)

Zeno, 88
Zizioulas, John, 76, 79–80

www.ingramcontent.com/pod-product-compliance
Lightning Source LLC
Chambersburg PA
CBHW051942160426
43198CB00013B/2257